PATHWAYS TO TEACHING SERIES
TEACHING METHODS

Charlotte Danielson
Danielson Group

Merrill
is an imprint of

Upper Saddle River, New Jersey
Columbus, Ohio

Library of Congress Cataloging-in-Publication Data

Danielson, Charlotte.
    Teaching methods / Charlotte Danielson.
        p. cm. — (Pathways to teaching series)
    ISBN-13: 978-0-13-513061-2
    ISBN-10: 0-13-513061-1
    1. Teaching—Methodology.   I. Title.
    LB1025.3.D363 2010
    371.102—dc22

                            2008047914

Vice President and Editor in Chief: Jeffery W. Johnston
Publisher: Kevin M. Davis
Acquisitions Editor: Meredith D. Fossel
Senior Managing Editor: Pamela D. Bennett
Senior Project Manager: Mary Irvin
Editorial Assistant: Nancy Holstein
Senior Art Director: Diane Lorenzo
Photo Coordinator: Lori Whitley

Cover Design: Jeff Vanik
Cover Image: Jupiter Images
Full Service Project Management: Aptara®, Inc.
Operations Specialist: Susan Hannahs
Vice President, Director of Sales and Marketing: Quinn Perkson
Marketing Manager: Jared Brueckner
Marketing Coordinator: Brian Mounts

This book was set in Garamond by Aptara®, Inc. It was printed and bound by Bind Rite Graphics. The cover was printed by Bind Rite Graphics.

Photo Credits: P. 3, Copyright 2001–2008 SMART Technologies ULC. All Rights Reserved; p. 11, Royalty-Free/Corbis/Corbis Digital Stock; p. 23, Corbis RF; p. 31, RAL Studio/Jupiter Images Picturequest–Royalty Free; p. 43, Comstock Royalty Free Division; p. 50, Comstock/Superstock Royalty Free; p. 60, IT Stock/Jupiter Images Picturequest–Royalty Free; p. 75, Anthony Magnacca/Merrill; p. 89, Photodisc/Getty Images; p. 97, Todd Yarrington/Merrill; p. 106, Frank Siteman; p. 121, Kathy Kirtland/Merrill; p. 128, Krista Greco/Merrill.

Pearson Education Ltd., London
Pearson Education Singapore, Pte. Ltd.
Pearson Education Canada, Ltd.
Pearson Education—Japan

Pearson Education Australia, Limited
Pearson Education North Asia, Ltd., Hong Kong
Pearson Educación de Mexico, S.A. de C.V.
Pearson Education Malaysia Pte. Ltd.
Pearson Education Upper Saddle River, New Jersey

Merrill
is an imprint of

www.pearsonhighered.com

10 9 8 7 6 5 4 3 2 1
ISBN-13: 978-0-13-513061-2
ISBN-10:   0-13-513061-1

As Lee Iacocca famously observed, "In a completely rational society, the best of us would be teachers and the rest of us would have to settle for something else." This sentiment captures what attracts committed educators into the profession, namely, the opportunity to engage in truly important work,—to make a difference not only in the lives of the students one teaches, but in the future course of the human race.

Teaching is enormously complex and challenging work; it is not for the faint of heart or for the uncommitted. It requires sustained effort over many years to acquire the skills, patience, and perseverance to take on the multiple challenges that present themselves. Teaching, in other words, merits the best human capital our society can muster in its service.

Astonishingly, in American society, the profession of teaching provides neither the financial rewards nor the status in society that its importance deserves. Those who enter the profession, therefore, do so from a deep commitment to the well-being of young people, and to the future of both their country and the world. It is to these educators that this book is dedicated.

PREFACE

Teaching is generally recognized as one of the most important professions anyone can enter. It is teachers, after all, who ensure that the next generation of citizens will acquire the knowledge and skills to lead productive and fulfilling lives, and be equipped to lead the nation and the world in solving the daunting problems facing humankind.

Teaching is also correctly regarded, certainly by anyone who has ever attempted it, as the most challenging work on the planet. Teachers must be responsive to multiple stakeholders—principals, parents, the school board, the larger community—while planning for the academic, social, and emotional well-being of the most important people of all: the students. And it's not a single student who commands a teacher's attention or even many students one at a time. No, it is many students *simultaneously*! Teaching is, in other words, daunting work; this is not a profession, as the saying goes, for sissies. When a professional educator states that "I'm just a teacher," the statement reflects an ill-founded modesty about the significance of the work.

Many institutions are devoted to the mission of helping teachers do their jobs well: the colleges and universities that prepare them, the mentors and coaches who support them in their critical first few years, the principals who offer guidance, and the professional development courses and workshops available for practicing educators to enhance their skills. But the truth remains that teaching is an extremely challenging profession and that teachers themselves must assume considerable responsibility for ensuring their ongoing learning about different aspects of their work: remaining abreast of developments in their subjects and how to bring these alive for students; pursuing ongoing developments in the organization of curriculum and matters of school practices such as scheduling and grading; and developing approaches to create learning environments that ensure the success of all students.

PURPOSE

The primary purpose of this book is to help educators (particularly those new to the profession) appreciate the many factors that influence the complex decisions they make every day in performing their professional duties. Its aim is to help them understand the complex factors at work as they plan and implement learning experiences for their students in such a way as to engage them in high-level learning. It makes explicit the many assumptions that undergird such decisions, enabling educators to address important issues openly and candidly.

It's important to recognize that such decisions are complex, bringing together in a teacher's mind the students and their backgrounds, the important learning that must be pursued, and, most important, recent findings regarding how students learn. Coordinating all these considerations into a single coherent plan of action is no small task.

Yet, teachers do it every day, many times a day. This book contributes to teachers' decision-making processes in such a way that the learning experiences they create (or adopt or adapt) for their students will yield the greatest possible success.

ORGANIZATION AND STRUCTURE

This book is intended as a guide to teaching for practitioners as they seek to understand their complex profession. It does not attempt to oversimplify the work of teaching—that would be a disservice to teachers. Rather, it attempts to provide, in plain, jargon-free English, an overview of the essential considerations of all teachers as they go about their work and ensure high-level learning for students.

Part 1 contains the "mental maps" for instructional planning, providing a summary of all the essential considerations that influence a teacher.

- Chapter 1 provides a summary of what we know about content: the imperative of high-level learning and why it's so important for today's students to be well equipped with the skills and knowledge that will bring them success throughout their lives. The chapter describes the many different types of learning outcomes we have for students (for example, knowledge, thinking skills, and collaboration) and provides a rationale for including them all in a well-balanced curriculum.
- Chapter 2 offers an overview of what we know about assessment, the different purposes to which assessment data are put and by whom, the different types of assessment (for example, formative and summative), and the challenges involved in aligning both the content and the assessment procedures with the outcomes being assessed. It also presents important examples of student work and discusses the insights teachers can gain from a careful analysis of student products.
- Chapter 3 provides a summary of what we know about student learning and the implications of this research for mobilizing student energy in the classroom.
- Chapter 4 takes a look at why students are motivated to invest huge amounts of energy in some pursuits (for example, mastering the skateboard) but are less interested in expending equivalent energy in school-related tasks.

    Chapters 3 and 4 together offer teachers the foundation for instructional planning that engages students in the high-level learning envisioned in Chapter 1 and assessed in Chapter 2.

Part 2 discusses the implications of the essential mental models described in Part 1 for detailed instructional planning. It provides suggestions for using what we know from Part 1 to design compelling learning experiences for students.

- In Chapter 5, teachers receive guidance in what is arguably the first responsibility of every teacher: knowing their students. It is essential, of course, to understand the typical characteristics of, for example, 10-year-olds. It is also essential to understand the backgrounds, communities, and school-related skills of this *particular* group of 10-year-olds in a teacher's class.
- Chapter 6 concerns the establishment of learning outcomes for students. It points out that learning outcomes are formulated at many different levels of detail, from the general program (what do we want our students to learn as a result of studying science?) to

courses (what are the desired learning outcomes for biology?) to units and then to individual lessons. Teachers are also reminded of the different *types* of learning outcomes and the possibility of coordinating or integrating learning outcomes from different disciplines into single units of study.

- Chapter 7 deals with the issues surrounding the design of assessments for particular units of study, as well as the challenges involved in creating performance assessments and their accompanying rubrics to analyze student work. It provides specific example of holistic as well as analytic rubrics and a commentary on the instructional examples from the Appendix.
- In Chapter 8, all the considerations described in the previous chapters are brought together in a discussion of what is at the heart of teaching: the design of engaging learning experiences for students. It is argued that because of the active nature of student learning, it is critical for teachers to be able to design activities and assignments that are intrinsically interesting to students and that yield the learning desired.

Part 3 deals with the implications of what we know about creating an environment for student learning.

- Chapter 9 explores the issues in creating a safe and challenging environment. Of course, the environment must be safe for students to take intellectual risks; they must feel that they can make a mistake without being penalized. But the environment must also be a challenging one in which students know that they must put forth their best effort in order to master complex material.
- Chapter 10 addresses management matters: the routines and procedures, the protocols for student conduct, and the performance of noninstructional duties. In this area, efficiency is the key to success, as is the involvement of students in every stage of planning and implementation.
- In Chapter 11, the many issues surrounding grading student performance are addressed, and recommendations are provided for an innovative approach to this sometimes contentions issue.

Part 4 addresses teachers' involvement beyond their own classrooms in the life of the school.

- Chapter 12 describes the imperative for teachers to participate in a professional community in their schools, to work collaboratively with their colleagues, and to contribute to the collective knowledge of the entire school.
- Chapter 13 explores the many opportunities for teachers to engage in leadership activities in their schools and beyond. Some of these opportunities are the result of teachers taking on a formal role, such as department chair or instructional coach. But others arise informally as teachers find that they have the time and the expertise to mobilize their colleagues around an area of need in the school.

Finally, the Appendix contains two detailed instructional examples, from different levels of schooling and different disciplines, that illustrate the major principles of this book. And the References and Additional Resources list a number of resources that interested educators can use to pursue the ideas and concepts presented in the chapters.

ACKNOWLEDGMENTS

I would like to thank the reviewers of my manuscript for their valuable insights and comments: Grant L. Holly, North Carolina State; Nicholas Bekas, Valencia Community College; and Susan Sheffield, Manatee Community College.

ABOUT THE AUTHOR

Charlotte **Danielson** is an educational consultant based in Princeton, New Jersey. She has taught at all levels, from kindergarten through college, and has worked as an administrator, a curriculum director, and a staff developer. In her consulting work, Ms. Danielson has specialized in all aspects of teacher quality and evaluation, curriculum planning, performance assessment, and professional development.

Ms. Danielson has worked as a teacher and administrator in school districts in all regions of the United States. In addition, she has served as a consultant to hundreds of districts, universities, intermediate agencies, and state departments of education in virtually every state and in many other countries. This work has ranged from the training of practitioners in aspects of instruction and assessment to the design of instruments and procedures for teacher evaluation to keynote presentations at major conferences. Clients for the development of materials and training programs include the Association of Supervision and Curriculum Development (ASCD), the College Board, the Educational Testing Service, the California Commission on Teacher Credentialing, and the National Board for Professional Teaching Standards.

Ms. Danielson is the author of a number of books supporting teachers and administrators. These include *Enhancing Professional Practice: A Framework for Teaching* (1996, 2007), the Professional Inquiry Kit *Teaching for Understanding* (1996), *Teacher Evaluation to Enhance Professional Practice* (in collaboration with Tom McGreal) (2000), *Enhancing Student Achievement: A Framework for School Improvement* (2002), and *Leadership That Strengthens Professional Practice* (2006), all published by ASCD. In addition, she has written several *Collections of Performance Tasks and Rubrics,* published by Eye on Education.

BRIEF CONTENTS

CONTENTS

INTRODUCTION: WHY THIS BOOK IS IMPORTANT

Teaching is extraordinarily important and complex work, yet for a variety of historical and economic reasons, it has never commanded the respect (or the compensation) taken for granted in other professions. However, the rewards of teaching are immeasurable; the knowledge that one can make a significant difference in a student's life, the challenge of conveying complex material to students, the gratification that follows a student's sudden understanding—all these provide a sense of significant meaning in the teacher's choice of career.

Those who enter teaching following other activities, whether achieving an advanced degree in a discipline, taking time to raise children, or pursuing another career, are making a conscious choice; they have not stumbled into teaching because of inertia or external expectations. These individuals are frequently motivated by a passion for the subjects they teach and a desire to share that passion with their students. They have decided that teaching is what they really want to do, and they set about realizing this ambition.

It's not uncommon, however, for idealistic teachers to begin their work in the classroom and face almost immediate disillusionment. The pressures are enormous—from colleagues, administrators, and the students themselves. The work never seems to be finished, and the travails of a novice may create a "sporting" environment for some students. They may regard it as a challenge to make life as difficult as possible for their teachers, engaging in a zero-sum game of dominance in which it is impossible for both parties to win. How to engage students in important learning, enlisting their extraordinary powers of intelligence and curiosity, is the subject and the promise of this book.

THE COMPLEXITY OF TEACHING

Everyone who considers the question acknowledges that teaching is enormously complex work. Various factors play into this complexity.

Professionalism

Of all the professions, teaching is arguably the most demanding and complex. As Lee Shulman (2004) has memorably written:

> The practice of teaching involves a far more complex task environment than does that of medicine. The teacher is confronted, not with a single patient, but with a classroom filled with 25–35 youngsters. The teacher's goals are multiple; the school's obligations far from unitary. Even in the ubiquitous primary reading group, the teacher must simultaneously be concerned with the learning of decoding skills as well as comprehension, with motivation and love of reading as well as

word attack, and must both monitor the performance of the six or eight students in front of her while not losing touch with the other two dozen in the room. Moreover, individual differences among pupils are a fact of life, exacerbated even further by the worthwhile policies of mainstreaming and school integration. The only time a physician could possibly encounter a situation of comparable complexity would be in the emergency room of a hospital during or after a natural disaster. (p. 258)

Teachers make hundreds of decisions daily, often under conditions of uncertainty. One of the challenges of those new to the profession is that they have a limited repertoire, which means that they may not have a "Plan B" to use even if a change is clearly needed. Sensitivity to the nuances of the classroom and the skill to respond with flexibility are aspects of teaching that develop with experience.

In addition, teachers are ideally members of a professional community in which colleagues develop a shared understanding of practice. One of the enduring problems of the teaching profession is that many teachers work in isolation, with relatively little meaningful contact with their colleagues. It is a mark of a professional culture, a culture of professional inquiry, that teachers have the opportunity to learn not only from their own practice but also from one another.

The Dynamics of Pedagogy

Every student has had a teacher who was extraordinarily knowledgeable about a subject but devoid of skill in conveying that knowledge to others. In other words, the individual could not *teach*. With such teachers, presentations may be too technical, using obscure words, or they may be unclear. Alternatively, classes may simply be *boring*, with no obvious reason for students to care about the subject.

Techniques used to teach science are very different from those employed in literature or mathematics. Bringing the material to life for students, engaging their intelligence and curiosity, is the essence of teaching. And although presenting content knowledge is essential for good teaching, it is not sufficient; the teacher must also enter the minds of students and determine what learning experiences will enable them to master complex material. However, it's not only the principles of pedagogy that must be mastered by the novice teacher, but *content-specific* pedagogy (using a term coined by Lee Shulman) as well.

Thus, it is essential for those new to the profession to devote attention to issues of instruction as distinct from knowledge of the content itself. What are the most recently developed approaches to teaching? How does one design learning experiences for students? The answers to these questions depend on understanding fundamental issues of cognition, motivation, and design—all addressed in this book.

The Challenges of Beginning Practice

Beginning to practice in any profession is difficult. In teaching it is particularly so, because there is no apprenticeship period during the training process. Granted, during their preparation program, most teachers will have completed a student teaching assignment designed to simulate the complex environment of teaching. However, there are many aspects of teaching that cannot be simulated. Until one is the teacher of record, they are simply not part of the program—for example, communicating with parents or referring a student for special services.

Furthermore, those entering teaching through an alternate route will usually not have had the clinical experiences included in most teacher preparation programs; they may be truly learning on the job. Unless they have embarked on an extensive program of professional reading, they may not be familiar with the profession's buzz words such as *differentiation, schemas,* or *cooperative learning.* Although all these terms have common-sense meanings and are accessible to novices, lack of familiarity with them can make the new teacher feel unprepared in the company of more experienced colleagues.

The Priority of Learning

When teachers begin their practice, they naturally think in terms of what teaching involves, that is, what they must do. Even principals and supervisors, when they evaluate or support teachers, frequently focus on the teacher's actions and behaviors.

The teacher's actions are not irrelevant, of course, to what is happening in the classroom. The teacher is the adult in the room and has created a learning environment for students. But teaching is not a *performance;* teachers are not putting on a show for students. Instead, they are creating conditions in which students learn. Sometimes this involves presenting information; sometimes it means establishing learning centers where students can work more independently. But underlying all instructional design is a focus on what the students are learning and how best to create the conditions for that learning.

Connecting with Students

The prospect of facing 25 students or more every hour of the day (and, at the secondary level, a different 25 students every hour) is daunting to those new to the profession. The teacher, who is only one person, may feel as though he or she is confronted with a crowd of young people. Indeed, most guides for new teachers are devoted to classroom management: how to organize the room, establish standards of behavior, and manage instructional groups. This is important information, but if it constitutes the teacher's entire repertoire of how to think about the classroom, it encourages a view that is too limited to yield good practice.

Instead, it is important for teachers, even new teachers, to recognize that their classes consist of individual students, individual people, individual learners, each with a unique set of interests, strengths, skills, and challenges. The challenge of teaching is to tune in to the *learning* of each student. It's not sufficient to say, perhaps breezily, "Oh dear, this is a slow class."

When adults recall their school experiences, it is the interactions with teachers that stand out in their minds. They can remember, sometimes after 40 years, a teacher's insulting comment or the way a teacher demonstrated confidence in their abilities. It's not a matter of style: Some teachers are stern; others are friendly and joke with their students. But teachers whom students recall with fondness after many years are those who demonstrated that they *cared* for them as individuals.

WHY THIS BOOK IS IMPORTANT

Given the complexity of teaching and the critical nature of teachers' work, it's essential that those new to the profession have available to them valid mental models for their work. They must understand the students they teach and how those students learn. They must understand the nature of the subjects they intend their students to learn and why those subjects are important. And most importantly, they must have the skills to design learning experiences that enable their students to engage in high-level learning of important content.

This book is intended to offer guidance to individuals new to teaching, both those engaged in a traditional preparation program and those entering the profession through an alternate route. It aims to provide new professionals with the tools they need to make wise instructional decisions on behalf of their students and to equip them to participate as full members of their professional community.

Part 1

WHAT WE KNOW

Every action taken by a professional educator is grounded in a series of beliefs: beliefs about how students learn, indeed beliefs about what is worth learning. Actions are influenced by teachers' sense of which students are capable of learning important content, and whether they are motivated on their own to do so or whether they require external inducements.

It's important to note that although teachers' beliefs are essential in shaping their actions, those beliefs, in general, are not stated explicitly. Most people's beliefs hover under the radar of conscious understanding or analysis, even while they influence, and even determine, action. For example, much of what constitutes a school's curriculum in mathematics at the middle school level consists of procedures for solving different types of problems. These might be problems about the area and perimeter of polygons, about converting decimals into fractions and vice versa, or about breaking numbers down into a series of prime numbers. Furthermore, homework assignments typically involve multiple examples of the different types of problems to solve, with students' completion of homework assignments contributing to their final grade. Implicit in these practices are beliefs about the nature of mathematics (it consists of a series of procedures), about how students learn mathematics (they learn the procedures by being taught them and then practicing them), and about their motivation for learning (they will practice the procedures only if rewarded, through the grading system, for doing their homework).

Each of these beliefs—about the nature of content, about how students learn that content (indeed, whether all students are capable of learning that content), and about the nature of student motivation—could be examined in terms of both their source and their validity. The beliefs outlined above reflect the cluster of attitudes toward school and the prevailing

1

practices evident in many schools. These beliefs and practices reflect, in turn, the experience that most adults—including most teachers—had as students in school. This means that adopting a different set of beliefs and actions might require a break from one's own experience, which, due to its prevalence, is comfortable.

However, on closer inspection, it turns out that many of the prevailing beliefs do not reflect current research findings regarding learning or the most recent policy recommendations regarding the important content that should be taught in schools. On deeper examination, it turns out that in order to make the significant improvements required of America's schools, all teachers (particularly those new to the profession) must not only understand important research findings, but must also determine how to put in place the implications of those findings.

Part 1 of this book describes important aspects of what we know about content, assessment, student learning, and motivation. Many of the findings, grounded in well-designed research studies, are considered common sense by many adults. For example, every parent knows about the drive to learn that propels young children. Some other findings are less well established in the general understanding and may even be counterintuitive, such as the need to use praise with care.

But a deep understanding of these research findings is critical for teachers if they are to promote high-level learning. The implications of these findings are described in Parts 2 and 3.

Chapter 1

What We Know About Content

Educators and policymakers, when deciding what students should learn in school, are confronted with a dizzying array of choices and dilemmas. The first of these concerns sheer volume; there is far more to be learned than can be absorbed by students during the time they are in school. But beyond the matter of quantity, there are decisions to be made at every step of the way. Many of these choices are made by state standards committees or district curriculum directors. But others are made by teachers themselves as they plan their daily lessons. This chapter outlines the issues involved in making those decisions.

DEMANDS FOR THE 21ST CENTURY

It would require breathtaking arrogance to predict the skills and knowledge that will be required of citizens of the world, or even of the United States, by the time today's elementary school students are finishing their working lives. Today's fourth graders will still be in the workforce in more than 50 years. Who could have predicted, 50 years ago, the profound transformations that have occurred in all aspects of life and work? Who could have foreseen that secretaries, who used to type and sometimes take dictation, would be managing (and even creating) complex databases? Who could have predicted that mechanics or farmers, in addition to acquiring deep knowledge in their specialties, would also be using intricate computer diagnostic equipment? Who would have guessed the world of information at our fingertips since the advent of the World Wide Web?

By the same token, who would be so presumptuous as to look forward 50 years and proclaim, with any degree of confidence, what specific knowledge and skills our current elementary students will need? What societal and economic changes await them? How can we, as educators, equip them to lead productive and rewarding lives? The only assertion one can make, with any degree of confidence, is that students will need the skills to continue learning in order to adapt to new conditions. And they will require the confidence to know that they can be successful in approaching an unfamiliar task. As has been pointed out endlessly since about 2000, the future will belong to those nations (and to companies within those nations) whose citizens have the freedom and support to use their imaginations to create new solutions to problems, some of which are still evolving. As Thomas Friedman has written:

> . . . when the world becomes this flat—with so many distributed tools of innovation and connectivity empowering individuals from anywhere to compete, connect and collaborate—the most important competition is between you and your own imagination, because energetic, innovative and connected individuals can now act on their imaginations farther, faster, deeper and cheaper than ever before. . . . Those countries and companies that empower their individuals to imagine and act quickly on their imagination are going to thrive. . . . These are oil wells that don't run dry. (*New York Times,* June 10, 2007)

The idea that jobs of the future would require skills profoundly different from those being taught in schools is not, of course, new. In 1990, the Secretary of Labor appointed the Secretary's Commission on Achieving Necessary Skills (SCANS) and asked it to examine the demands of the workplace and whether today's young people are capable of meeting those demands. These necessary skills included:

Competencies

- ***Resources.***   Allocating time, money, materials, space, and staff
- ***Interpersonal Skills.***   Working on teams, teaching others, serving customers, leading, negotiating, and working well with people from culturally diverse backgrounds
- ***Information.***   Acquiring and evaluating data, organizing and maintaining files, interpreting and communicating, and using computers to process information
- ***Systems.***   Understanding social, organizational, and technological systems, monitoring and correcting performance, and designing or improving systems
- ***Technology.***   Selecting equipment and tools, applying technology to specific tasks, and maintaining and troubleshooting technologies

The Foundation

- ***Basic Skills.***   Reading, writing, arithmetic and mathematics, speaking, and listening
- ***Thinking Skills.***   Thinking creatively, making decisions, solving problems, seeing things in the mind's eye, knowing how to learn, and reasoning
- ***Personal Qualities.***   Individual responsibility, self-esteem, sociability, self-management, and integrity

The SCANS report, while it influenced educational discussion and debate throughout the 1990s, had little enduring effect on state content standards and assessments. Its findings were indisputable; its implications were far-reaching and would have required much of schools to transform themselves into high-performing organizations imparting high-level skills. It has not happened yet.

Of course, the demands on schools to prepare students for their future lives extend well beyond equipping them to participate in the evolving economy; they include supplying the skills and dispositions for them to participate fully as citizens. Thomas Jefferson noted in the 18th century that a democracy depends on an educated citizenry; otherwise, people are vulnerable to the promises of demagogues and dictators. In order to vote intelligently, people need to be able to evaluate the claims and arguments made by those seeking office; they need to be able to distinguish between empty promises and careful analysis; and they need to be able to ask hard questions of their public servants. Furthermore, since our judicial system depends on citizen juries, every individual must be equipped for that important role. The case was made by Justice Leland deGrasse in a New York case:

> A capable and productive citizen doesn't simply turn up for jury service. Rather, she is capable of serving impartially on trials that may require learning unfamiliar facts and concepts and new ways to communicate and reach decisions with her fellow jurors. . . . Jurors may be called on to decide complex matters that require the verbal, reasoning, math, science, and socialization skills that should be imparted in public schools. Jurors today must determine questions of fact concerning DNA evidence, statistical analyses, and convoluted financial fraud, to name only three topics. (Decision rendered on January 1, 2001, and reported in the *New York Times*, January 11, 2001)

Of course, most school curricula are organized according to traditional academic disciplines: mathematics, English, science, and so on. These constitute the ways in which knowledge is structured and how students are introduced to the accumulated wisdom of Western culture. To the extent that these disciplines encompass important knowledge, such an approach is unlikely to change. In addition, however, educators must ensure that students have access to the essential aspects of those disciplines (essential concepts, critical and creative thinking, collaboration skills, etc.) that will be needed to propel them through their later lives.

These issues are not simple, and they serve to frame the debate in state departments of education, district curriculum offices, and school departments. But in their considerations of what is worth learning, educators and policymakers must address a number of issues. These issues are described in the following sections.

THE STRUCTURE OF THE DISCIPLINE

Every discipline has its own particular structure, with essential concepts and principles, prerequisite relationships, and connections with other disciplines. These factors largely provide the structure by which students engage with that content.

Concepts and Principles

Every discipline consists of essential concepts and principles; many of these are woven throughout the different topics introduced during students' study of that discipline. For example, the concept of pattern is critical to an understanding of mathematics; it may be introduced to 5-year olds, and it is critical to trigonometry. In the study of history, the concepts of revolution and counterrevolution help explain many events of the past 1,000 years, and scientific inquiry in biology is largely organized around the concepts of structure and function. In the study of literature, students are exposed to the different genres (poetry, fiction, etc.), and they learn, in language arts, the skills of writing both fiction and nonfiction. Every discipline has its *strands*, which serve to organize systematic study, and to permit increasing complexity and depth as students move through the grades.

Many states and professional organizations, in their articulation of content standards, have done a commendable job of defining the essential concepts and principles for each of the major disciplines; some states' standards are highly detailed, whereas others are more general. Regardless of their level of generality, such content standards offer important guidance to educators as they develop their own curricula and design learning experiences for students. Rather than spending valuable (and scarce) instructional time on trivia, it's important that both teachers and students devote their energies to important learning.

Prerequisite Relationships

Not only is each discipline organized around a number of essential concepts and principles, but these concepts and principles are also related to one another, and understanding of one concept depends on understanding of others. For example, until students understand the concept of addition, they can't tackle multiplication. In learning a modern language, the content of each year's study builds on that of previous years.

The *concept* curricula, such as science and social studies, are less dependent on prerequisite relationships than are the *skills* curricula of reading and mathematics. But even in science and social studies, the same concepts will be addressed many times throughout the years at increasingly complex and sophisticated levels. For example, the idea that plants obtain their food from the sun is frequently introduced to very young children when teachers invite them to explore the conditions under which classroom plants thrive compared to those under which they struggle. But the full concept of photosynthesis is complex and is studied in far greater depth in high school biology class. Similarly, the concepts of democracy and monarchy may be introduced in elementary school, but the nuances of a democracy and how it is different from a republic, and the questions of whether it's possible to call a country a democracy if its elections are somewhat less than open and fair, will wait until high school.

The challenge for those writing curriculum documents, then, is to ensure that the standards reflect the critically important concepts within each discipline and that the curriculum is structured in such a manner that students are not expected to master a particular concept until they have learned other prerequisite concepts.

DIFFERENT TYPES OF LEARNING OUTCOMES

Curriculum standards typically cover the full range of concepts and skills important to each curriculum area and are organized in such a manner that students are equipped to learn each concept as it is introduced. But this range of outcomes includes different *types* of learning outcomes, all of which are important to a comprehensive grasp of the discipline. These include knowledge, of course, but also reasoning and the skill of working collaboratively.

The different types of learning outcomes are described below; those who design curricula draw on each of these types in their work.

Knowledge

Much of what is learned in school consists of knowledge, and indeed, one of the marks of a well-educated person is that he or she knows a lot. But even knowledge consists of some subcategories, each of which warrants consideration.

- *Factual Knowledge.* Factual knowledge is exactly as it sounds, consisting of facts, dates, definitions, rules of grammar, and the like; factual knowledge implies "knowing that." Every discipline contains some factual knowledge—for example, the date of the Mexican-American War, the boiling point of water, the author of *Great Expectations*. There was a time when factual knowledge comprised the vast majority of what students learned in school.

  More recently, educators have argued that factual knowledge is less important, because facts can easily be looked up in reference sources or on the Internet, and that students should not stuff their heads with unrelated bits of information. However, it remains true that although many facts can be retrieved easily, much information must reside in people's minds, to be called upon as needed. Furthermore, without a wide range of facts at their disposal, individuals cannot hope to relate those facts to one another and to discern patterns among them. For example, it is not until one has studied a number of revolutionary movements across history that one can recognize similar characteristics in contemporary conflicts.

- *Conceptual Understanding.* *Conceptual understanding* refers to the knowledge of concepts, principles, trends, patterns, and the like. Thus, an understanding of buoyancy involves far more than simply memorizing its definition; indeed, one could recite a definition, or choose the correct definition from a list of possible definitions, without being able to explain the concept. Cognitive psychologists now recognize that factual knowledge without conceptual understanding is hollow and vulnerable to being forgotten. It is the conceptual understanding that supplies the contextual web for the facts, enabling students to make sense of the facts they learn.

- ***Procedural Knowledge.***   Unlike factual knowledge, which consists of knowing *that*, procedural knowledge consists of knowing *how* to do something. Therefore, a student with procedural knowledge of algebra can factor polynomials or solve equations with two unknowns; another knows how to organize his thoughts for an essay. But in order to be permanent, procedural knowledge requires a firm grounding in conceptual understanding. Only after students understand the concept of a prime factor will they be able to perform the procedure of factoring polynomials.

  It is unfortunately the case that procedural knowledge can, particularly in mathematics, mimic conceptual understanding. For example, students can be taught by rote how to "get the right answer" in problems involving subtraction with regrouping. But only when they have a deeper, and far more powerful, understanding of the structure of a base system of numeration are they able to engage in more complex problem solving involving number theory. So, although students can be coached, through the memorization of mathematical procedures, to get the right answer when the problems are simple and routine, their understanding is not sufficient to enable them to engage in the study of mathematics or to derive the satisfaction that comes with powerful knowledge.

Skills

The second principal category of content is that of skills, the ability to *do* various things. And, as with knowledge, there are several different types of skills.

- ***Thinking and Reasoning Skills.***   Every compilation of valued learning outcomes for students includes attention to thinking and reasoning: discerning the difference between fact and opinion, collecting and analyzing information, formulating and testing hypotheses, predicting outcomes, and so on. These reasoning skills may be developed in any area of the curriculum and, indeed, can serve as unifying principles.

  Employers frequently report that the skills involved in problem solving are critical to success on the job. Most tasks cannot be completely routinized; those that can are increasingly assigned to robots. And because many problems are ill-defined, problem analysis is frequently an essential component of problem solving. Before a problem can be solved, in other words, it must be understood.

- ***Communication Skills.***   The centerpiece of the elementary curriculum is literacy, the skill of deriving meaning from the printed word. Until one can read, much other learning is inaccessible. So, it's not surprising that elementary schools devote considerable time to developing the reading skills of their students. And when those students' first language is other than English, the task is made far more difficult.

  But communication skills don't end with reading. One of the most frequently heard complaints from university faculty and employers is that recent graduates possess inadequate communication skills in both speaking and writing. And with the pervasive use of e-mail, the lack of writing skills is on daily display in many workplaces.

There is no substitute for clear speaking and writing; frequently, the presence (or absence) of such communication skills is a reflection of clear thinking (or its absence). And, as with thinking and reasoning, attention to communication need not be restricted to a single part of the curriculum (typically English and language arts); instead, these are skills that can and should be developed throughout the school day.

- ***Social Skills.*** The ability to work well with colleagues is an essential skill in virtually all workplaces, as well as being vital for personal fulfillment. Thus, many curriculum documents include in their desired outcomes the skills of collaboration. Such skills include the ability to listen carefully to others, understand another person's point of view, keep group work focused on the task at hand, and others. The emergence of teams in many workplaces has shone a spotlight on the importance of such collaborative skills; very few jobs, and fewer households, enable a person to function as a sole practitioner.
- ***Learning-to-Learn Skills.*** As noted above, students entering school today will still be in the workforce 50 years from now; if one contemplates the dramatic changes that have taken place over the past 50 years, it's clear that the competencies that will be required for success in tomorrow's world are currently unknown and indeed unknowable. Not only have skills evolved, but entire professions have emerged, fueled primarily by the revolution in electronic communication. No sensible person would attempt to predict the specific skills needed to advance, or even survive, in the second half of the 21st century. This relentless shifting of the terrain explains why it is essential for today's students to develop the skills of learning—acquiring new information, making connections between old facts and new ones, discerning patterns, and learning new skills.

Aesthetics, Disposition, and Ethics

Although most of the outcomes of schooling are assumed to involve the acquisition of knowledge and skills, including social skills and thinking skills, many schools make a deliberate effort to broaden their goals to include other areas. For example, the English curriculum includes not only the skill of analyzing a novel's plot structure, but also appreciating the author's use of imagery. Likewise, many schools, in their treatment of the settlement of the American West include the view of the native inhabitants, to whom it appeared more as an invasion. Treatments of civics topics and analyses of historical events include attention to fundamental American values such as fairness and justice, equal rights, and the like. And most schools work to instill the habits of perseverance and open-mindedness in their students. None of these areas is likely to be included on a formal test, but all are important to a school's success in achieving it broadest aims and to students' success in life.

OVERLAP

Curriculum documents produced by states and school districts elaborate the different learning outcomes of each type described above, for each discipline, independently of other disciplines. They are typically produced by experts within each field and reflect the structure of each subject. However, there is tremendous overlap among the disciplines, particularly in the areas of reasoning and communication skills.

For example, the concept of a recurring pattern emerges in mathematics, to be sure, but also in science, social science, and literature—as in patterns of events in history and science or behavior patterns of a character in literature. The skill of classifying is, of course, central to biology, but also to literature (referring to works according to their different genres), social science (the differences between a parliamentary or representative democracy and a direct democracy), and mathematics (comparing prime and composite numbers). Thus, when students have learned how to recognize patterns, or how to classify objects or ideas, those skills are applicable across the curriculum. Similarly, the skills of communicating one's understanding are virtually universal, involving many of the same, but some discipline-specific, attributes.

Moreover, the skills of argumentation are universal. That is, when explaining events in history or science or in interpreting a piece of literature, students must be able to "make a case": present a position and back it up with evidence. Students who are skilled at argumentation will ask "How do you know?" and they can answer that question for positions of their own. This skill is essential throughout life and is equally important when presenting an argument and when analyzing and evaluating others' claims—for example, those of candidates for political office or the advertising claims for products. Everyone engages in argumentation in the course of daily life, but not everyone does it well; politicians and advertisers know that they can make unsupportable claims and that few will challenge them.

These *process* skills transcend the curriculum—they are universal, not belonging to any particular academic discipline. And because they play a role in virtually every subject, in most state curriculum documents they are presented every time they apply, which is to say, in every discipline. This phenomenon results in considerable redundancy, which educators, when they plan their units and lessons, must sort out.

However, this sorting out is best done by teachers working together or through a school's curriculum process. For example, the skill of classification is part of many disciplines; it underlies students' understanding of number (prime and complex numbers) and of language (beagles are a type of dog, and dogs are a type of mammal), to say nothing of science and social studies. But classification involves more than dividing objects or concepts into discrete groups. In many cases, groups may overlap (for instance, the red square belongs in the group of squares and also in the group of red objects) or one group may be embedded in another (for instance, both the United States and Canada are part of a larger category called *North America*).

Thus, the complex skills of classification and the different types (discrete, overlapping, and hierarchical) must, at some point, be taught to students. And because they are not unique to any one discipline, they may be taught either in one of them or independently. (The danger, of course, is that because they are not unique to any particular discipline, they won't be taught at all or will be taught superficially in many subjects.) But once students have been introduced to the concepts of classification, their future learning can build on the ideas, enriching that learning.

Summary

Decisions regarding what students should learn are complex and are grounded in many considerations. Teachers themselves decide, on any given day, what to teach, as described in Chapter 6. But those decisions are not arbitrary; rather, they are based on issues of what constitutes important learning, what is appropriate for the teacher's own students, and the curriculum as mandated by the state and district.

Chapter 2

What We Know About Assessment

It's one thing to decide what's worth learning and what we want students to learn in school; it's quite another matter to ascertain that they have, in fact, learned it. Indeed, unless we can ensure that students have learned important content, state and district curriculum standards are meaningless. They are merely words on paper, subject to anyone's interpretation.

Assessment design, in fact, plays a more important role than simply serving as a check on student mastery; the assessments serve to define the curriculum standards themselves. For example, a standard in intermediate-level mathematics might state that students can "select and apply a variety of appropriate problem-solving strategies (e.g., 'try a simpler problem' or 'make a diagram') to solve problems." Few would argue with such a standard but, on its own, it tells us little about what exactly is expected of students. That is, most readers would expect an elaboration in the form "the student could solve a problem such as the following: . . ." in order to fully understand the standard. Otherwise, they are left to wonder how challenging the problem should be. Can it be solved in one step or might more than one step be needed? What numerical operations should be included?

PURPOSES OF ASSESSMENT

Much has been written and many conferences have been conducted on the subject of assessment. But missing from many of these articles and discussions is clarity about purpose. Why is student learning assessed? For what aim? For which audience? When these questions are answered clearly, it's possible to design assessments that are both valid and valuable. When they are not, teachers muddle through, doing the best they can but sometimes confronted with conflicting demands. Therefore, clarity about purpose, combined with an understanding of the options, is essential.

There are two principal purposes of assessment:

1. Assessment *of* learning, that is, assessment whose purpose is to determine whether students have learned some specific content in the curriculum
2. Assessment *to guide* learning, that is, assessment that assists both teachers and students in determining the next steps to be taken in instruction

In addition, there is a third purpose of assessment:

3. Assessment for *teacher* learning. That is, when teachers engage in assessment, they find that they become more knowledgeable about their students and about their own teaching.

From the point of view of teachers, the important consideration is those aspects of student assessment that they control or at least influence. And for those aspects of assessment that are determined by others, it's important for teachers to know how to make use of the information provided.

Assessments Developed by Teachers (Either Individually or with Colleagues)

The role of assessment in teaching has been recognized for some time; the critical role that teachers play in both designing and interpreting assessment results has been more recently understood.

ASSESSMENT *OF* LEARNING (<u>SUMMATIVE</u>)   The first, most obvious, and most widely ac-knowledged purpose of assessment by teachers is to <u>determine the extent of student learn-</u><u>ing in the curriculum.</u> It answers the questions "Have they learned it? If so, how well?" In general, such *summative* assessments are better if designed by teachers collaboratively; this approach ensures the best collective thinking. Furthermore, to the extent that the assess-ments define the outcome of teaching (e.g., in the case of a jointly administered end-of-course test), assessments guarantee that all students in a particular school are exposed to es-sentially the same content. This ensures that everyone in the school understands what is included in, for example, Algebra I or 10th-grade English. Teachers use the information from these assessments for several distinct, though related, purposes:

- To assign grades, particularly at the secondary level, that reflect (or should reflect) the degree of content mastery in a course.
- To allow entry to advanced courses. For example, in some schools, students must demonstrate a certain quality of writing in order to enroll in advanced-placement (AP) English; in other schools, a student who wants to take a second year of Spanish must demonstrate mastery of the content of first-year Spanish.
- To qualify a student for advanced standing or access—for example, to use the power equipment in a wood shop or to determine which student will serve as the concert master of the school orchestra.

When designing summative assessments (those intended to reveal the extent to which stu-dents have mastered the curriculum), teachers must ensure that the approach taken is suit-able for the outcomes of the curriculum. For example, if the curriculum states that students will learn to write for a variety of purposes and audiences, a multiple-choice test would not accomplish this. Similarly, if the curriculum calls for understanding the concept of buoyancy, selecting the correct definition from a list of definitions would not reveal understanding. This aspect of assessment will be addressed in a later section of this chapter.

ASSESSMENT *TO GUIDE* LEARNING (<u>FORMATIVE</u>)   In addition to developing summative assess-ments, teachers have multiple opportunities daily <u>to discover, in a more informal manner, how</u> <u>students are progressing in their learning and what, specifically, should be done next</u>. This use of assessment is called *formative* and can be employed by both students and teachers.

To understand the formative use of assessment, it's instructive to contrast it with a more traditional approach. In traditional instruction, the class addresses a topic (e.g., frac-tions) for a certain period of time and then moves on to another topic (e.g., decimals). At the end of the unit on fractions a test is administered and graded, and the grades are entered in the grade book. In this approach, the assessment signals the end of instruction on fractions.

However, formative assessment, rather than occurring at the *end of* instruction, is *integral to* instruction. That is, students may have been learning about fractions for a number of days, with brief assessments conducted along the way. These are not marked and used to determine a grade; rather, they are intended to provide information to both the teacher and the students. If they are designed to be diagnostic, with a view to revealing which students understand which parts of the curriculum (and if they don't understand it, what they seem to understand instead), then the next day's lesson may be shaped accordingly.

The skilled use of formative assessment is not an afterthought; like all aspects of good teaching, it must be planned at the outset. Formative assessment is, above all, di-agnostic. Teachers can discern, from the manner in which students perform, what they have mastered, what learning is still in development, and which learning is inaccessible to them at the present time. This information is essential in planning future lessons. If students are taught to analyze their own work, they can also become partners in the enterprise.

ASSESSMENTS DEVELOPED BY EXTERNAL AGENCIES (STATE DEPARTMENTS OF EDUCATION, DEVELOPERS OF AP OR IB [INTERNATIONAL BACCALAUREATE] COURSES, COLLEGE-ADMISSIONS BODIES)   In addition to the assessments they design themselves, teachers obtain information from a variety of external sources, over which they have very little, if any, control or influence. However, even these external assessments may provide information for teachers if they are skilled in extracting it.

External assessments are administered for a range of purposes:

- *To Certify Individual Students.*   There are many situations in which individual students' learning must be certified as sufficient. Although some of these are organized by teachers, others are mandated by state agencies—for example, to determine eligibility for graduation or for the next level of schooling. In some states, students must pass a high school proficiency test in order to graduate; in others, students are not permitted to enter high school prior to demonstrating achievement in the middle school curriculum. These tests are typically mandated and scored by state departments of education.

- *To Evaluate or Accredit Schools.*   In many states, schools are evaluated by the performance of their students on the state's standardized achievement tests. In today's environment of high-stakes accountability, the results of such tests carry enormous implications, including the takeover of failing schools. (Of course, when the results of tests are used for high-stakes decisions regarding schools, there are considerable—in some cases irresistible—temptations for both teachers and principals to find ways to cheat. This has, unfortunately, been documented.)

- *To Determine Teacher Effectiveness.*   In some jurisdictions, the results of externally mandated assessments are used to determine teacher effectiveness. In order to claim that their work is effective, the argument goes, teachers must be able to demonstrate that they have a measurable impact on student learning. This is a powerful argument, one that, in its broad statement, is irrefutable. However, in order for a teacher's effectiveness to be fairly assessed using student achievement data, those data must be calculated according to the value-added for which an individual teacher can reasonably be held responsible. That is, there are many factors outside school—and many factors within a school but beyond the control of individual teachers—that affect student learning. Teachers may be reasonably held responsible for the difference between a student's achievement at the end of the period (at the end of the year, for example) and what it would have been expected to be based on that student's prior rate of learning. Such determinations are possible, but they depend on sophisticated statistical techniques and can only be used when there are valid assessments for the learning under consideration. Thus, the effectiveness of teachers of most high school courses in science, mathematics, social science, and even English, to say nothing of other languages and the performing arts, cannot be evaluated using such an approach.

Assessment for Learning by Teachers

Lastly, an important outcome (if not a design purpose) of assessment is to encourage insights by teachers, that is, to promote teacher learning. By analyzing student work in response to well-designed assessments, teachers can derive important information on the success of a lesson and on the progress of individual students. There are several distinct, although related, mechanisms through which this occurs.

DESIGNING SUMMATIVE ASSESSMENTS   When teachers design summative assessments, particularly with colleagues, they must clearly define their learning outcomes and decide what would constitute evidence of student understanding. This is not a simple matter; it's tempting to think that one can simply write a test for a unit and that this is the end of the matter. However, depending on the learning one wants students to demonstrate (particularly if it includes not only facts and procedures, but also skill in analyzing information or interpreting events), the assessments must reflect those more complex outcomes. Designing such assessments is valuable for teachers and results in significant learning.

DESIGNING FORMATIVE ASSESSMENTS   Designing formative assessments is not the same thing as monitoring student learning during instruction. Monitoring, and adjusting an approach based on what one observes, is critical to good teaching. But formative assessment goes much further, requiring teachers to determine, in advance, what successful and ongoing learning would look like and how to know that this is happening. Alternatively, if students are not learning, it is important to determine which elements of a lesson need to be retaught or which students are eligible for more advanced work.

Designing such formative assessments is important professional work, best achieved, like all professional work, by teachers in teams. It requires deep understanding of the content to be learned and familiarity with the strengths (and weaknesses) of students in the class. As teachers acquire skill in this area, they become highly attuned to the dynamics of learning and are able to respond sensitively as needed.

TYPES OF ASSESSMENT

There are several different types of assessment, which are described below.

Tests

Every teacher (and every student) is familiar with tests; they are administered to ascertain students' proficiency in important learning outcomes. Even when teachers incorporate other, newer assessment methods into their teaching, they don't abandon tests, largely because tests are an efficient way to determine the level of student knowledge and skill.

Unlike other assessments, tests are administered under what are known as *testing conditions*. Testing conditions usually include the following:

Limited time.   Students are asked to complete a test within a certain amount of time, typically a class period, although it may be more or less than that. Critically, though, unless students have special needs, the amount of time permitted to all students is the same.

Limited (or no) resources.   In a test, students are not permitted to look at their notes, or a text, or at any other resources that might provide assistance. This ensures that what students produce on a test reflects only their own understanding and explains why students' writing answers to predicted questions on their hands, for example, is rightly regarded as a serious violation of testing conditions. Of course, teachers sometimes administer what they call *open book* tests, the very name suggesting that under normal conditions, students are not permitted access to their books.

Individual effort.   During a test, students are not permitted to consult with peers or look at other students' papers. Like the rule forbidding access to materials, this ensures that what students produce on a test reflects their own understanding and not that of their classmates.

In addition to the conditions governing test administration, there are two different types of tests: select and constructed response.

SELECT TESTS   As its name suggests, a *select* test requires that students select the best answer from the choices provided. The most common form of a select test is multiple-choice, although it can also consist of true/false or matching items. In a select test item, students can often improve their success rate by eliminating obviously wrong answers, thereby demonstrating an apparently increased level of knowledge.

Tests composed of select items can be scored quickly, which makes them attractive to teachers. It's possible to compare students' answers to an answer key and quickly ascertain which items have been answered correctly. And if the *distracters*—the wrong answers in a multiple-choice test—are cleverly constructed, it's even possible for teachers to derive some diagnostic information about students' understanding from the mistakes they make. However, multiple-choice, true/false, and matching test items are not easy to construct in such a manner that the wrong answers are plausible to students and yet are unambiguously incorrect.

CONSTRUCTED RESPONSE TESTS   In a *constructed response* test, students create, or "construct," their own answers, responding to an open-ended question in their own words. Essay questions are constructed response items that ask students to demonstrate their understanding of a topic. In general, constructed response items are more demanding of students and reveal more about what they know than do multiple-choice items. Of course, because it takes longer for a student to answer an essay question than a multiple-choice item, any test can include fewer of them, implying that the range of what can be assessed through essay questions is smaller than what may be tested through multiple-choice items.

There are other limitations to constructed response items. Students who write well may receive a higher score than others who know as much but cannot express themselves well. Furthermore, some students, particularly as they progress through the grades, learn how to answer essay questions using many words but saying very little. However, in general, teachers can ascertain far more about what a student knows from a constructed response question than from a multiple-choice item.

Many tests administered by teachers are a combination of select and constructed response items. This permits teachers to sample students' knowledge over a wide range of content and to explore their understanding more deeply in a few areas.

Figure 2.1 is an example of the range of understanding, among six students in a typical class, of a constructed response question intended to elicit understanding of the concept of one half.

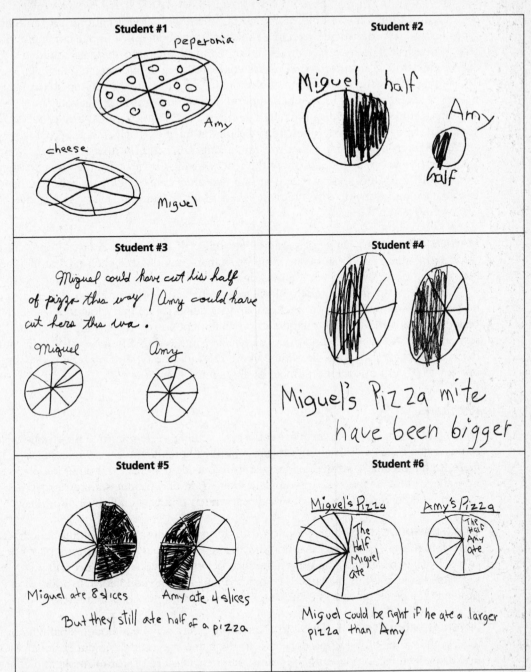

FIGURE 2.1 Using a constructed response question such as the one in the mathematics performance task, teachers can learn much about their students' grasp of a concept. Here, six students indicate their understanding of the concept of.

Figure 2.1 is an example of the range of understanding, among six students in a typical class, of a constructed response question intended to elicit understanding of the concept of one half. The student samples illustrate the insights into students' thinking a teacher can acquire from constructed response as compared to multiple-choice questions.

Using a constructed response question such as the one in this mathematics performance task, teachers can learn much about their students' grasp of this concept.

In a more traditional approach, a number of different figures would be presented, some with one half shaded, others with a different fraction (such as one third or four fifths) shaded. Students would be asked to draw a ring around those that represented one half. Such an approach will, indeed, show the teacher which students in the class possess what is, arguably, a limited understanding of one half: they can *recognize* a half. But, as is clear from the examples that follow, there are layers of understanding; student work offers teachers a window into those layers.

MATHEMATICS TASK   Directions: Miguel ate one half of a pizza. Amy ate one half of another pizza. Miguel said that he ate more pizza than Amy did, but she said that they both ate the same amount. Who do you think is right?

It is clear that there is much information to be acquired from these student responses. Of course, some students (5, 6, and probably 4) demonstrate that they understand the concept of one half and that the quantity in one half depends on the size of the whole. But the responses of students 1, 2, and 3 are particularly interesting. They reveal that the students believe that other aspects of the situation are relevant: the type of pizza, whether the cut is horizontal or vertical, and the number of slices into which it is cut.

Products

Sometimes teachers ask students to produce something to demonstrate their skills or understanding of a concept. These products are typically not made under testing conditions; that is, there is no time limit, and students may consult outside materials and other people. Students may take as long as they like to complete their work, and products are evaluated according to established criteria. They are of two types: written products and physical products.

WRITTEN PRODUCTS   Written products used for assessment may be of any length, ranging from a short essay completed as a homework assignment to a far longer term paper or report of a science experiment. The only difference between a written product and a constructed response test item is that the latter is completed under testing conditions. In addition, a written product may be assigned to be far longer than would be possible on a test.

PHYSICAL PRODUCTS   Physical objects are *things;* they may be a model, a painting or sculpture, or a diorama. Physical products are, as the name suggests, three-dimensional; they take up space. Students produce them to illustrate their mastery of, for example, a technique in woodworking or metalworking, or in carving, or their sense of design and composition.

Like written products, physical products are not completed under testing conditions, although they may be done in school, particularly in the visual and industrial arts, because needed tools and materials are located there.

Many science projects are a combination of written and physical products; students may write a report and create a model demonstrating a scientific phenomenon or experiment. Such projects, if the guidelines require explanations of the phenomena, can provide teachers with rich insights into what students know and can do. This information is even richer if students must also explain their projects orally and respond to questions from both the teacher and other students.

Products created outside of school, whether they are written or physical or a combination of the two, present challenges for the teachers examining them, however, due to the difficulty of establishing authenticity. Most teachers have had the experience of trying to evaluate a project while being unsure of whether the work was the student's alone, or the extent to which the student had assistance from parents or older siblings. Similarly, the term papers submitted by some students reflect a far higher standard of writing than those students demonstrate in in-class assignments, suggesting, at the least, some serious editing by others. Therefore, although products are an important source of information about student learning, most teachers don't rely on them exclusively to assess student performance, particularly if the stakes are high. That situation merely encourages some students to seek outside assistance, even when they know that they should not.

Performance

Teachers can also assess student knowledge and skill not by what they *produce,* as in a test or a product, but by what they *do.* This category of assessment is referred to as *performance,* and it may be either structured or spontaneous. (In this context, the term *performance* does not necessarily mean that the performance is rehearsed, as in a theatre production. Students may have practiced what they are to do, but not necessarily.) In general, a performance is ephemeral; once it is completed, there is no trace left. Of course, a skit or a speech may be videotaped and evaluated later, but performance is typically a one-shot affair.

STRUCTURED PERFORMANCE   In a structured performance, students perform in front of others, usually their classmates, although possibly a panel of evaluators. The structured performance may be a speech on an assigned topic, a debate, a Spanish dialogue, or playing a musical passage. Of course, students may be making a joint presentation, but each student plays a role in the final effort. Structured performance is essential for assessing student skill in, for example, a speech class. In an out-of-school context, the quintessential structured performance assessment is the driving test; in every state, applicants are required to demonstrate that they are able to actually drive a car. Passing a written test is not sufficient.

SPONTANEOUS PERFORMANCE   Students also demonstrate their knowledge and skill in spontaneous ways in the classroom in how they read aloud, or work with peers, or through the questions they ask and the responses they provide. However, because of its very nature, spontaneous performance is unstructured; teachers can't count on its revealing important information about student learning. For this reason, spontaneous performance is used, at most, as a supplemental form of assessment. On the other hand, by creating behavior checklists, teachers are able to make their informal assessments as revealing as possible regarding what students know and can do.

These different types of assessment, with several examples of each, are provided in Table 2.1.

TABLE 2.1 Forms of Assessment

Test		Product		Performance	
Select	**Supply**	**Written**	**Physical**	**Structured**	**Spontaneous**
• True/false test • Multiple-choice test	• Short-answer questions • Essay test	• Essay • Term paper • Lab report	• Sculpture • Model	• Student reading • Speech or presentation • Musical performance • French or Spanish dialogue	• Group work

MATCHING ASSESSMENTS TO LEARNING OUTCOMES

As noted in the descriptions of each assessment type, certain ones are more suited to some types of learning outcomes than to others. For example, for outcomes concerning student skill in writing, only actual writing will do. This would take the form of either a written test or a written product, depending on whether or not it is important that the assessment be administered under testing conditions. Similarly, to assess student skill in reasoning and problem solving, a constructed response item on a test would serve, as would a written task (a product).

It will be recalled from Chapter 1, "What We Know About Content," that educators establish their aims for student learning across a wide range of types of content; none are more valuable than others, but they are profoundly different from one another. These differences suggest both a range of instructional strategies and (our purpose in this chapter) a range of approaches to assessment.

The types of learning outcomes described in Chapter 1 are:

Knowledge

- *Factual Knowledge:* knowing *that* something is the case, such as the events in a novel, the capitals of different nations, or the chemical symbol for iron.
- *Procedural Knowledge:* knowing *how* to complete a procedure, such as factoring polynomials, cleaning glassware, or organizing a term paper.
- *Conceptual Understanding:* possessing a flexible understanding of complex concepts and their interactions, such as the permanence of number, the relationship between buoyancy and density, or the essential characteristics of democracy and its difference from a republic.

Skills

- *Thinking and Reasoning:* being able to relate concepts to one another—for example, to formulate and test hypotheses, analyze data, and compare and contrast one idea with another.
- *Communication:* the skills of reading, writing, speaking, and viewing. The lower level skills of decoding, grammar, and mechanics consist of purely routine skills,

whereas higher order communication skills, such as interpreting text, require the use of thinking and reasoning skills as well.

- *Social Skills:* being able to get along with others, to listen actively, and to treat others with respect. In addition, there are facilitation skills of working collaboratively, helping a group stay on track, and being able to summarize a group's progress.
- *Learning to Learn:* the ability to acquire new knowledge and learn new skills when necessary. The most vivid example is from computer technology, but the need to engage successfully in ongoing learning is pervasive.

Aesthetics, Disposition, and Ethics

These are the clusters of vital attitudes and appreciations, such as the ability to recognize the beauty in an elegant mathematical proof, the inclination to maintain an open mind, and a sense of justice and fairness in interactions.

When one contemplates the many different types of learning outcomes and the different approaches to assessment, it becomes clear that some types of assessment are more suitable than others to different categories of learning. This is summarized, with examples, in Table 2.2.

It should be noted that the only type of learning outcome for which a multiple-choice test is completely appropriate is factual knowledge; for other (arguably more important) types of learning outcomes, more complex forms of assessment are essential. Furthermore, when teachers use other forms of assessment, it's not sufficient to have an answer key; answers are not simply right or wrong. Rather, there are degrees of excellence on all important criteria. Thus, for evaluating student performance on, for example, an essay, it's necessary to use a scoring guide, or rubric, which identifies the critical elements of a good essay and provides a description of each element at different levels of proficiency.

TABLE 2.2 Designing Appropriate Assessments

Types of Learning Outcomes	Test		Product		Performance	
	Select	Supply	Written	Physical	Structured	Spontaneous
Knowledge						
Factual knowledge	XX	XX	XX		X	
Procedural knowledge	X	XX	X			
Conceptual understanding	X	XX	XX	X	XX	X
Skills						
Thinking and reasoning	X	XX	XX		XX	X
Communication		XX	XX		XX	
Social skills					X	XX
Learning to learn		XX	XX	XX	XX	XX
Aesthetics, disposition, and ethics		XX	XX		XX	XX

Note: A double XX denotes a completely appropriate form of assessment; a single X denotes a partially appropriate form.

The issues surrounding the design of assessments, and the creation of rubrics or scoring guides with which to evaluate student performance, are discussed in Chapter 7, "Assessing Student Learning."

Summary

Student assessment is a complex topic with a number of different considerations for teachers to understand. As teachers design learning experiences for students and determine how they will assess that learning, it's important for them to be aware of the many issues involved, particularly the alignment of their assessment methodologies with their learning outcomes. The practical details of assessing student learning, and of using assessment both for evaluation of students and in promoting student learning, are addressed in Chapter 7.

Chapter 3

What We Know About Student Learning

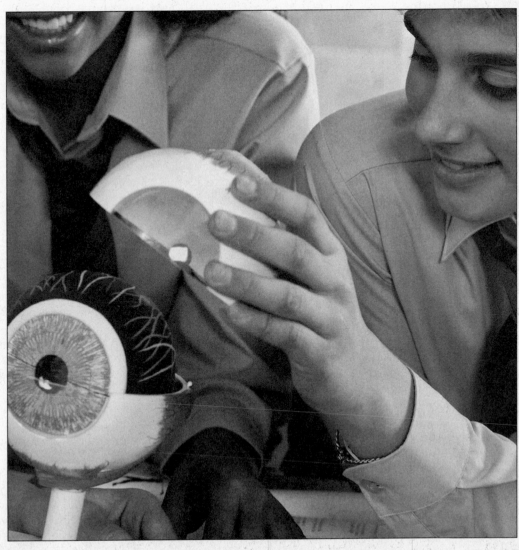

It's impossible for teachers to arrange for student learning if they don't possess a workable mental model of how that process occurs or, worse, if their mental model is inaccurate or outdated. Both are, unfortunately, possible, resulting in frustration for the students and the teacher.

Professional understanding of how students learn has progressed, not always smoothly. Current convictions now reflect, with some modifications, those held by educators in the mid-20th century in what was called at the time *constructivism.* This was to distinguish it from *behaviorism,* which also had many adherents; the two implied radically different instructional strategies.

COMPETING VIEWS OF KNOWLEDGE AND LEARNING

The education community is not unified in its understanding of knowledge and learning. Although a consensus has been developing in recent years, there are threads of several distinct and competing views held by educators, which, over the past century, have enjoyed varying degrees of influence. These are briefly described below.

Behaviorism

In the behaviorist view of cognition, a person's state of knowledge at any point consists of that person's behavior. Thus, someone who knows French can speak French; a person who knows about American history can discuss it knowledgeably with others. A person's state of cognition, in other words, consists of the sum total of his or her behavior; the behavior both defines what a person knows and how he or she manifests that knowledge.

Thus, in the behaviorist view, since knowledge consists of behavior, learning occurs when behavior changes. One's dog has learned not to beg at the dinner table when family members no longer must tell him "no," that is, when he has "learned," because of training, to stay in the next room. Similarly, a child can be said to have learned multiplication when he or she can recite the multiplication facts accurately. Students demonstrate that they have learned about democracy when they can select the correct definitions from a list of possible options. In other words, if knowledge is reflected in behavior, then learning is reflected in a change in behavior.

The behaviorist perspective has enormous implications, of course, for how teachers organize their classrooms and their lessons to promote learning. To the extent that learning consists of a change in behavior, then what is needed to cause, and to verify, learning is to arrange for students to demonstrate a change in behavior by, for example, answering questions correctly. How they come to be able to demonstrate such a change is less important than the fact that they do so. Therefore, a behaviorist orientation may lead some teachers to use instructional techniques that focus on drill, memorization, or knowledge of procedures.

The behaviorist view of learning was popularized in the 1960s by B. F. Skinner, primarily through research with animals. He demonstrated that dogs could learn to associate a bell's ringing with the subsequent arrival of food. When those same dogs later salivated (a response) on hearing the ringing of the bell (a stimulus), they could be said to have "learned" that a bell "causes" food to appear. Dubbed the *stimulus-response* (or *S-R) theory,* this view of learning had, for time, a considerable impact in schools.

In schools following a behaviorist tradition, learning was thought to consist of instructing students so that they could provide the correct response (answer) to a stimulus (question). The students' minds were not thought to be "actors" in this process; rather, they were empty vessels to be filled. Along similar lines, teachers were not considered to be active players, but rather conveyors of information. Thus, scripted lessons and "teacher-proof" materials could be developed by experts and provided to teachers for implementation.

Constructivism

A different view of learning, more developmental and cognitive, has evolved over many years (even decades) and has a long tradition in the writings of Dewey, Vygotsky, and Piaget. This view of learning is grounded in a constructivist rather than an associative approach to knowledge. That is, what is known does not consist of a response to a stimulus, manifested in behavior, but that which is understood or *constructed* by the individual.

This more complex view of knowledge implies that an individual's demonstration of that knowledge is correspondingly more complex than in a behaviorist approach. Thus, to demonstrate knowledge of democracy, for example, it's not sufficient to select the correct definitions from a series of choices; one must be able to explain the concepts in one's own words, relate them to similar but different concepts, and provide an example from everyday experience. Understanding, from a constructivist perspective, consists not of the repetition of facts and procedures, but the application of knowledge from one situation to another that is unfamiliar.

This constructivist concept of learning takes a very different view of the mind than does the behaviorist concept. Rather than being thought of as an empty vessel to be filled, the mind is conceptualized as an intensely active agent. Rather than the quiet and cooperative students envisioned by many teachers in their private images of the perfect classroom, this view sees children as highly active, curious creatures who, given a choice, would rarely sit down.

Of the two views of learning (behaviorist and constructivist), the weight of research in cognition has, in the past several decades, decisively swung to the constructivist perspective; learning is now recognized to be a result of purposeful activity by a mind making sense of its complex environment. This is not to argue that there is no place for the rote learning of facts and procedures, but rather to recognize that these facts and procedures must be embedded in complex understanding. This constructivist conceptualization has been bolstered by advances in neuroscience and cognition; it will be the focus of the remainder of this chapter.

CONSTRUCTIVISM: AN EXPLANATION

Understanding how high level learning and advanced cognitive skills are acquired by students, and how to develop the intellectual capabilities needed for understanding and processing information, are at the heart of the advanced instructional skills required by teachers. Understanding the underpinnings of learning—of how students construct their understanding—is the foundation of these instructional skills.

Constructivism, as a theory of learning, has a long and respected pedigree in cognitive psychology, particularly as reflected in the writings of Dewey, Vygotsky, and Piaget. It reflects the idea that students, when they enter our classrooms (and even earlier, while they are still at home), create their own understandings of the world. Adults assist in this process, to be sure, but the key to understanding learning is to appreciate how students themselves encounter new ideas and integrate them into their prior understanding. An implication of this idea is that different individuals, depending on their previous understanding and cognitive structures, will acquire different understanding even from the same activity or presentation. Individuals acquire understanding based on what their preexisting knowledge and cognitive structures allow them to absorb——regardless of a teacher's intentions or the quality of an explanation. The bedrock idea of the constructivist view is that it is the *learner* who does the learning; learning does not result directly from what teachers do but from what students do. Although this idea might seem simplistic, it is not; it will be further explored in the following sections.

The Active Nature of Learning

Even casual observation of young children provides anecdotal support for the constructivist view of students and their minds. Watching young children figure things out is one of the fascinations of parenting; young children are constantly in motion, intensely exploring everything they encounter, whether it is a plastic toy, an animal, or the paper wrapping covering a gift. They explore how things look, feel, and taste, and the noises they make. Even the mistakes children make reveal that their minds are constantly active. When a preschool child refers to animals in the field as *sheeps,* he demonstrates that he has figured out the method of adding an *s* to a word to form a plural. The fact that the rule does not apply in this case merely serves to illustrate the child's mind at work.

It should be noted that with very young children, parents do little that could be called teaching. When babies lift themselves up on their knees and hands, their parents don't get down on the floor and urge their children to "watch me" while they demonstrate how to crawl. No: Babies figure out how to crawl, and how to do much else, on their own, without direction or explicit teaching by adults. This drive for learning and development is absolutely hard-wired; young children are learning machines.

Indeed, young children's curiosity can be quite exhausting to their parents and teachers. The constant question "Why?" and its repetition each time an explanation is provided eventually drives many adults to declare that "That's just how it is!" Most preschool children are constantly busy exploring both the physical and the human worlds. And they learn a lot. Indeed, if one considers the sophisticated learning that accompanies a child's acquisition of language, it's difficult not to respect the accomplishment.

For an infant lying in a crib, the world is a cacophony of noise, and yet, by about 18 months, babies have a modest repertoire of words. What do they do? First, they learn to distinguish voices from other sounds, such as dogs barking, doors shutting, or glasses clinking. Then they begin to associate certain sounds with certain people or events, the first typically referring to the child's parents or other caregivers, or to routine events such as eating or sleeping. They learn to recognize and then to reproduce the words for, *milk* and *juice,* moving on from nouns (*dog*) to verbs (*dog runs*) to adjectives (*brown dog runs*) and finally to adverbs, prepositions, and other parts of speech.

All in all, it's a remarkable achievement, and virtually every child learns language, initially without any formal instruction. Thus, when the child walks into the kindergarten classroom and says "Good morning," one can conclude that she is a successful learner because she has learned to walk and talk, two highly complex achievements. Thus, children's minds, after the first few months of life, are not blank slates or empty vessels. Instead, even very young children construct theories of how the world works, and they make predictions based on their experience to this point. For example, young children figure out, on their own, the basic principle of gravity: that when an object is dropped, it will fall to the ground. They don't yet understand the general principle that explains the phenomenon of falling objects, but they have derived the rule that governs their observations. Students, when they encounter phenomena, must integrate those events into their current understanding of the world. This they do seamlessly, often without any intervention from an adult.

John Dewey expressed the concept of student natural activity as well as anyone in 1907 (p. 17):

> The child is already intensely active, and the question of education is the question of taking hold of his activities, of giving them direction. Through direction, through organized use, they tend toward valuable results, instead of scattering or being left to merely impulsive expression.

It's not, then, that teachers must motivate students to learn; they are already intensely motivated. The challenge is to channel children's natural energies toward productive ends, toward conceptual understanding of important content, toward the acquisition of lifelong skills.

The Level of Cognitive Structures

As children mature, they see the world and interpret events in it in profoundly different and well-researched ways. The most comprehensive account of children's development of thinking and logic was produced by Jean Piaget in the mid-20th century, and although certain aspects of his findings have been updated, the basic principles remain intact. Piaget discovered that as children mature, they interpret the world in significantly different ways, shifting from reliance on appearances, to an understanding of logic as it applies to physical objects, to the eventual use of proportional and hypothetical thinking. These shifts in thinking have an important influence on how children understand the world and what aspects of a traditional school curriculum they can understand (as distinct from memorizing and regurgitating) at any given time.

Young children attribute human-like emotions to inanimate objects and will report, for example, that the clouds are "angry." Primary school–age children's minds are overwhelmed by their perceptions, resulting in, for example, a conviction that a spread-out group of counters contains more objects than the same number arranged in a more compact pile. Such developing concepts affect how children understand, in particular, science and mathematics. Until about 8 years of age, children don't possess stable concepts of all the building blocks of mathematics and science: number, length, weight, mass, volume. They will declare, with conviction, that there is more water in a tall, skinny glass (it has just been poured from one container into another) than in a short, broad glass. Their judgment is overwhelmed by the perception that in the tall container it looks like more; therefore, it must be more. Only later can they appreciate that no water was added and none was taken away; even though it *looks* like more, it *can't* be more. This evolution in thinking represents the triumph of logic over perception, and it occurs in every facet of life. Until it occurs, teachers can't assume that their students' understanding of, in this case, volume, is stable; such stability develops over time and through experience.

Students' cognitive structures are indeed *structures*. When a child is at one level of understanding, perhaps as a 6-year-old with an unstable concept of number, as new ideas are presented, they are incorporated into that structure. Thus, the child may not be sure that 8 remains the same quantity when it is divided into 3 + 5 or 4 + 4 or 8 + 0; he may believe that these represent different quantities, making the memorization of number facts meaningless rote learning. The structures themselves change only when the child is confronted with experiences that cannot be accommodated by existing structures, forcing a revision.

Developing structures make important content accessible to students as they grow older. For example, students in intermediate grades are able to speculate on how a situation appears from the point of view of another person, an indispensable skill in understanding both literature and history. And adolescents can develop a highly evolved sense of ethics and possibility, enabling them to explore questions in history regarding, for example, what might have happened if an event had occurred in a different manner, or whether an individual in history or literature did the right thing and why. Older students are able to form hypotheses about the likely outcomes of a scientific investigation and can think several steps ahead in a problem in mathematics.

The universal and enduring patterns of cognitive development have important implications for teachers and developers of curriculum materials, and they suggest a rationale for a "spiral" curriculum. The American history to which students are exposed in the 5th grade is absorbed in a very different manner from the same facts revisited in the 8th or the 11th grade. To be sure, the facts may be memorized by 10-year-olds, but those same facts will be *understood* in very different ways by older students. When teachers are sensitive to these evolving patterns of development of cognitive structures, they are able to create learning experiences for their students that both reflect and stretch their understanding.

Prior Experiences

Every child who enters school has experienced thousands of events; these provide the raw material for what is to be learned in the more formal setting of the classroom. Teachers know that if they can make connections with students' prior experiences, the concepts they are trying to impart will be more readily understood than if they are presented in isolation.

Some experiences, of course, are culturally or class based. Children from affluent families are more likely to have traveled, or to have attended theatrical or musical events, than are poor children. Children who have spent time on a farm or hiked in the wilderness bring those experiences with them to school. Some children have never seen clothes drying on a line, whereas it is a common sight for others.

Much of what is learned in school is formalized and abstracted from common knowledge. For example, many children are familiar with the phenomena of the inside of a car becoming very hot on a cold but sunny winter day and water sitting in a hose becoming hot to the point of burning. A teacher introducing the principles of passive and active solar energy can use these experiences to help students understand those concepts. Experienced teachers will search for such background events in presenting new material to students.

Student Misconceptions

Of course, not all past experiences support formal school learning; some actually impede it. For example, children's experience with walking on the earth may make it more difficult for them to believe that the earth is round. Many teachers have encountered students who know that the "right" answer is that the earth is round but don't really believe it. Students have similar misconceptions about many other topics, particularly in the sciences. Many, for example, believe, even following detailed instruction in photosynthesis, that plants derive their food from the soil rather than, as they have been taught, from the sun. Many others, even those who have undertaken a detailed study of astronomy, believe that the summer is hotter than the winter because the earth is closer to the sun in the summer. (In fact, it is the tilt of the earth, not its proximity to the sun, that determines the seasons; otherwise, how could the seasons of the Northern and Southern Hemispheres be reversed?) But the tenacity with which many students hold on to their misconceptions, and may effectively hide them from their teachers, can create barriers to learning that surface only when students experience difficulty learning something that depends on the misunderstood concepts. Other learning is counterintuitive for students. For example, preschool children learn that 6 is larger than 4. But 1/6 is not larger than 1/4. It requires considerable conceptual teaching to help students understand why that is the case.

IMPLICATIONS FOR CURRICULUM AND INSTRUCTION

Given the complexity of learning, teachers can't simply "march through" a curriculum provided by their school or through a text series. Given that their goal must be student *understanding* of that curriculum—its knowledge, concepts, and skills—they must be able to apply what they know about learning, about how students achieve understanding, as they design daily learning experiences.

A constructivist approach does not imply that there is never a role for a teacher's lecture or for student memorization. Indeed, students can actively construct meaning from a lecture, although it's sometimes difficult for a teacher to distinguish active engagement with a lecture from daydreaming; vigilance and monitoring of understanding are needed. Similarly, there are times when memorization of facts is appropriate. Once a child's concept of number is secure, once he knows, for example, that every time five objects are combined with three objects the result is *always* eight objects, the number facts may be memorized.

Nor does a constructivist approach suggest that student activities should always include physical objects; students can work as mindlessly with concrete materials as with symbols on a piece of paper. What is necessary is that learning, rather than simply being "hands-on," is "minds-on." It is the mental activity that is important, not the physical. These ideas will be more fully developed in Chapter 8, "Designing Learning Experiences."

Of course, the work of designing learning experiences depends on what is to be learned: Different types of learning outcomes suggest different approaches; the methods used will differ according to the characteristics of the content. As described in some depth in Chapter 1, "What We Know About Content," there are several distinct types of content that students are asked to learn. Some of them are facts, others are procedures, and still others represent conceptual understanding. In addition, we ask students to be proficient in various aspects of creative and critical thinking: designing a scientific experiment, writing an original essay, or interpreting a passage in literature. We also hope that our students will become proficient in working collaboratively with others and in understanding situations from various perspectives. These different categories suggest different approaches to the way material is presented to students and what they are asked to do in order to learn it.

These different types of content are all legitimately part of a school's curriculum. If the only important type of learning in school were factual knowledge, then students could be asked to simply memorize it, and they could be tested on their recall of important facts. Instructional methods could consist entirely of rote drill, and assessments could rely exclusively on multiple-choice items. However, because all the different categories of content are important in the school's curriculum, instructional and assessment practices must reflect the demands of the full range of curricular outcomes. And in order to do that, educators must understand how students learn.

Summary

A critical question related to success in school is this: How do students come to understand important concepts in the different curricular areas of the school's program? How does that understanding develop? In order to answer those questions, one must appreciate how children learn, spontaneously and independently, as well as in the formal school setting.

Educators' understanding of how students learn has developed over the past century and is now consolidated. People learn through the active construction of meaning, based on their developing cognitive structures and their experiences. The implications of this constructivist view are profound, with important consequences for how students are introduced to important concepts in school, how they engage with those concepts, and how they integrate their understanding.

Chapter 4

What We Know About Motivation

INTRODUCTION

Teachers are understandably keenly interested in this question: What accounts for student motivation, that is, what makes students do (or not do) what we ask of them? In a classroom, after all, there are many more students than teachers, and if they are in high school, they may be physically bigger as well. So, why should they do what we ask of them? Why do they not rebel? Why do they not mutiny? Of course, some schools, or some classes within other schools, are out of control; chairs are thrown or, less violently, students are inattentive or defiant. However, students and their parents have a right to expect, at the very least, that schools be orderly places; teachers, in private visions of their classrooms, imagine eager students actively engaged in learning. Students cannot learn in a chaotic environment.

Furthermore, learning challenging content requires hard work and discipline on the part of students; to think that learning to write well or master trigonometry is easy is a fantasy. Even when lessons are well designed, even when explanations are clear, learning requires a certain measure of intellectual elbow grease. Why do students do it? Why, in some classes, do students willingly take on important and difficult challenges, whereas in others they are lethargic or, worse, rebellious? What do some teachers do differently? What do they know about students?

A casual glance around most schools and classrooms would lead one to conclude that the prevailing belief underlying most practices is that students are motivated by striving for rewards and avoiding punishments. Most elementary school teachers make liberal use of happy faces, gold stars, and the like. Some even institute elaborate token economies in which students earn the right to privileges, such as extra recess time or a pizza party on Friday. It is tacitly assumed that the work students are asked to do in school is, well, work, and that they will do it only with the promise of getting something they value. In high school classrooms, a frequent question from students is "Does this count?" or "Will this be on the test?" The answer will help students decide whether to make a serious commitment to do the necessary work.

Furthermore, posted classroom rules and teacher syllabi frequently spell out the procedures that govern interactions between teacher and students and the consequences for violations of the rules. That is, students' names may be written on the board as a first warning, then a check mark placed by the name on a second infraction, with a third resulting in going to a time-out space or the principal's office. In relation to schoolwork, homework handed in after it is due is given only half the credit of homework handed in on time. The entire enterprise of school appears to be informed by behaviorist notions of reward and punishment, with students, in effect, bribed to complete assignments or study for tests.

And yet, there are classrooms, familiar to all students and teachers, in which students willingly take on difficult challenges. They make a commitment to their work; they think of interesting questions to pursue; they are, in other words, fully engaged. What accounts for the difference? What is known about student motivation that can shed light on this situation and enable all teachers to release the inherent energy they know is present in all students for the learning at hand?

EXTRINSIC VERSUS INTRINSIC MOTIVATION

The question of whether students are motivated by extrinsic factors (gold stars, grades, etc.) or intrinsic factors (satisfaction, a feeling of competence, etc.) is vigorously debated in schools. Most of the policies and practices in schools support the idea of extrinsic motivation.

However, that view does not square with even casual observations of young children; no one has to reward a 3-year-old for exploring her environment. In fact, most children are so eager to learn new things that they must be restrained to protect them from dangers (such as running into the road) that they don't yet understand.

In order to understand extrinsic and intrinsic motivation, it is helpful to begin with what is known through ordinary observation.

- Young children are highly motivated to learn new things; they display extraordinary energy in the pursuit of understanding. Preschool children explore their surroundings with energy that is quite exhausting to their parents—wandering off, experimenting with piling things on top of each other, and so on. No one has to offer a treat to a young child to encourage her to master a new skill; in fact, learning to walk offers a telling example. If children were interested only in moving from one place to another as fast as possible, they would probably continue crawling, because initially, walking is much less efficient. Yet, all children do learn to walk; the developmental drive for learning is irresistible. As an additional example, every parent is familiar with the young child's insistence that "I can do it *myself!*" The drive of every child to achieve mastery and competence is irrefutable.
- Older children pursue their interests with energy that is breathtaking, even in the face of discouragement. For example, they persist in improving their skill in skateboarding even when they fall off regularly. Children who become involved in playing an instrument, taking photographs, or playing baseball pursue these interests with intense commitment. Most adults marvel at the time children devote to collecting baseball cards or practicing lay-ups. This dedication of time, and the intense discipline required, is motivated by almost purely intrinsic factors. Naturally, some students may want to have a skill to show off to their friends, so the approval of peers adds an extrinsic element to what is primarily an intrinsic motivation to excel.
- Computer games are other activities in which students engage with seemingly unlimited energy, even when they are "wiped out" periodically. In fact, it appears that the wipe-outs, and the opportunity to begin again with a clean slate, is one of the features that makes these games so appealing. Young people playing computer games are competing only with themselves; they strive to improve their performance against their own past record. Furthermore, they are not labeled as failures because they lost an earlier—and possibly easier—game.
- Students don't need incentives to volunteer for the school play, or for athletic teams, or for a jazz band, or to work on the school newspaper, even when such activities require a major investment of time beyond the demands of school. And because students are eligible for these activities only by demonstrated competence, they develop their skills in order to measure up.
- Some students are motivated to work hard by the prospect of getting high grades or by the fear of failure. These are typically the students who have a pattern of success and who regard failure as an anomaly. Students with a history of poor grades tend to have a more defeatist attitude; they don't expect to receive high marks and are therefore not outraged by low ones.

Psychologists have conducted numerous experiments to measure the relative strength of extrinsic and intrinsic influences on behavior. Not surprisingly, both influences are important, but their relationship with each other is interesting, with enormous implications for teachers. Psychologists have found that, in general, extrinsic motivation tends to drive out intrinsic motivation. That is, many activities are intrinsically interesting to young children, such as drawing with felt-tipped markers. But in a famous experiment, Greene and Lepper found that as soon as children were offered a reward for their pictures, they lost interest in drawing (stated in Sergiovanni, 1992, p. 24). This finding has been confirmed in many other studies, leading researchers to conclude that although people initially engage in an activity because they enjoy it, once rewards are offered, they work for the rewards. That is, the extrinsic motivation supplants the intrinsic one.

Another vivid example is cited by Richard Deci (1995), one of the preeminent scholars on motivation. He finds wisdom in an old Jewish fable:

> It seems that bigots were eager to rid their town of a Jewish man who had opened a tailor shop on Main Street, so they sent a group of rowdies to harass the tailor. Each day, the ruffians would show up to jeer. The situation was grim, but the tailor was ingenious. One day when the hoodlums arrived, he gave each of them a dime for their efforts. Delighted, they shouted their insults and moved on. The next day they returned to shout, expecting their dime. But the tailor said he could afford only a nickel and proceeded to hand a nickel to each of them. Well, they were a bit disappointed, but a nickel is, after all, a nickel, so they took it, did their jeering, and left. The next day, they returned once again, and the tailor said that he had only a penny for them and held out his hand. Indignant, the young toughs sneered and proclaimed that they would certainly not spend their time jeering at him for a measly penny. So they didn't, and all was well for the tailor. (p. 26)

Deci points out that "the 'rewards' linked to intrinsic motivation are the feelings of enjoyment and accomplishment that accrue spontaneously as a person engages freely in the target activities. Thus, feeling competent at the task is an important aspect of one's intrinsic satisfaction. The feeling of being effective is satisfying in its own right, and can even represent the primary draw for a lifelong career" (p. 64).

School is far more enjoyable for both students and teachers if students find satisfaction in what they are asked to do. It is much more fun to channel students' natural drive to learn into productive directions than it is to convince lethargic or alienated students to engage in unpleasant tasks. Steering energetic students is a more satisfying challenge for teachers, and more rewarding for students, than establishing a system of carrots and sticks to yield the results one is seeking.

CONTRIBUTORS TO INTRINSIC MOTIVATION

Teachers, then, must understand the factors that provide the impetus for intrinsic motivation so that these factors can be incorporated in the classroom. What causes the natural curiosity and energy that are, with luck and skill, built into classroom life?

Fortunately, the answer to this question is relatively straightforward, with consensus findings having emerged from the research of many scholars over a number of decades. Once the essential physical demands of food, clothing, and shelter are met, all human beings are motivated by powerful psychological needs. These needs have been identified and described by William Glasser, Edward Deci, and Robert White, among others. They are summarized below.

- *Making Connections with Others: Belonging.*   For teachers, it's not difficult to recall, from their own student days, the importance of one's friends and how critical their approval was. Dan Goleman, in *Emotional Intelligence* (1995), found that social isolation is roughly twice as detrimental to health as smoking. All societies, from ancient times on, have established punishments including banishment and exile. Early literature is replete with examples of such isolation being used as the most extreme punishment, short of execution, that could be meted out.

    Many adults have painful memories of being shunned by people they admired or being isolated from others. Teachers know that for some students, posturing in front of others or acting as the "class clown" is done primarily to gain approval, even at the risk of disciplinary action from the teacher. Notes between students are, in some classes, freely passed; students devote considerable energy to maintaining these "conversations" with their friends and teachers find themselves obliged to intercept the notes, thwarting students' efforts to connect with their peers. (The advent of text messaging has merely contributed another technique to what has been an issue in schools for years.) Furthermore, teachers know that, because isolation from others is so painful for students, the time-out room must be used sparingly.

    On a more positive note, researchers have found that when students are engaged in a task that will benefit others, they devote a great deal of energy to it. For example, when a group of first graders were creating story books and drawings to share with others, their teacher had to make a rule: "No leaving recess early to go back to class to work on your book" (Cognition and Technology Group at Vanderbilt, 1998, p. 61). That is, making a contribution to others is a powerful motivator and has been found to promote recovery in individuals suffering from depression; it helps all persons to develop feelings of worth and value.

- *Competence, or Mastery.*   Everyone has experienced the "high" that accompanies the attainment of a difficult goal such as the mastery of a challenging skill. And the more difficult it is, the more satisfying the feeling of accomplishment. It is surely this drive for competence that explains children's perseverance in using the skateboard or perfecting the lay-up. Understanding difficult academic content carries the same rewards, whether it is graphing the sine curve or speaking fluently in another language. The confidence of being able to say "Ask me anything!" before a test in school is very powerful, and its attainment is highly motivational.

- *Autonomy, or Freedom.*   No one enjoys being told what to do; one of the tricks of raising children is to ask them to make a "choice" from among necessary activities, such as "Would you like to go to bed now or in five minutes?" When adults recall their most meaningful experiences in school, they frequently remember those in which they selected the topic or the approach, as in a science project. Furthermore, when students choose what they are going to do and invest energy in pursuing it, they typically achieve a great deal of incidental learning, which neither they nor their teacher could have predicted.

- *Intellectual Curiosity.*   Adults and children alike respond to an intellectual challenge, whether it is offered in school, or as a newspaper crossword puzzle, or in a book of Suduko exercises. Such challenges are not relevant in any important sense, that is, they don't connect with anything else one is trying to accomplish. But they are fun and satisfying to master. It is the fun that is appealing; very few people can resist the challenge of a puzzle. Curiosity itself is what motivates people to engage with the puzzle; satisfaction accompanies a successful solution.

Sergiovanni proposes another way to look at the interplay between intrinsic and extrinsic motivation. He writes: "The traditional motivational rule—'what gets rewarded gets done'—has its place, but by itself is neither powerful nor expansive enough to provide the kind of motivational climate needed in schools. One alternative to this rule is 'what is *rewarding* gets done.' The work gets done, and it gets done without close supervision or other controls. The sources of motivation are embedded in the work itself" (1992, p. 26).

It should also be noted that mobilizing students' intrinsic motivation provides an important counterweight to the widespread practice of teachers enlisting student cooperation through the exercise of raw power. It's an undeniable fact that teachers have far more power than do students. They hold the students' futures literally in their hands, from deciding who to call on in class, to handing out various rewards such as praise, gold stars, or good grades, to withholding privileges such as free time or recess. But teachers find that when they rely on such power to force compliance, they become sucked into battles that are difficult to win; many students achieve stature among their peers by standing up to the power of an unpopular teacher. It's far more productive to avoid the power struggles altogether by enlisting students' natural energy for learning.

VIEWS OF INTELLIGENCE

Another important contributor to discussions of motivation is the views held by different individuals (students as well as their parents and teachers). The question to be considered is "What is intelligence, and how does it affect learning and motivation?" The answers matter.

Carol Dweck (2000, 2006), a social psychologist at Columbia University, has conducted a number of studies designed to explore these issues. She has posited two views of intelligence—fixed or malleable. Naturally, these attitudes represent a continuum, but the ends of the scale are well defined.

The *fixed-trait* view is that intelligence is something one is born with; any individual has only a certain amount of it. The *malleable-trait* view, on the other hand, holds that intelligence is something one develops through hard work and diligence. Intelligence, in other words, is not a fixed trait, but something that can be cultivated through learning and effort. "It's not that people holding this theory deny that there are differences among people in how much they know or in how quickly they master certain things at present. It's just that they focus on the idea that everyone, with effort and guidance, can increase their intellectual abilities" (Dweck, 2000, p. 3).

Somewhat surprisingly, Alfred Binet, the creator of the first intelligence test, held the malleable view of intelligence. He wrote:

A few modern philosophers . . . assert that an individual's intelligence is a fixed quantity, a quantity which cannot be increased. We must protest and react against this brutal pessimism. . . . With practice, training, and above all, method, we manage to increase our attention, our memory, our judgment, and literally to become more intelligent than we were before. (1909/1975, pp. 105–106)

The implications for students of these different views and their attitudes toward school (and especially their resilience when they encounter the inevitable difficulties) are profound. Those who hold the entity, or fixed-trait, view of intelligence worry about how much of it they have. They need to look smart or at least not look dumb. Therefore, such students are less likely to push themselves in trying to master challenging content. As Dweck (2000, p. 3) states, "the entity theory, then, is a system that requires a diet of easy successes. Challenges are a threat to self-esteem." Furthermore, when students holding an entity theory of intelligence encounter challenges, their response is one of helplessness; they give up easily.

Students who hold the malleable view of intelligence, on the other hand, are far more resilient and mastery-oriented. They eagerly take on challenges, and when they encounter obstacles, they are far more persistent in their approach. Dweck's research revealed another important and somewhat surprising finding: Students' views of their intelligence affected their success in making the transition from elementary to middle school. For many students this is a challenge, as they move from the intimate setting of an elementary classroom to the larger, more impersonal environment of a middle school. Dweck found that students who held the malleable view of intelligence made the transition easily and even thrived, whereas students with the fixed view struggled.

IMPLICATIONS

The critical message from the literature on motivation is that it's important to structure the classroom and the design of learning activities in such a way that they capitalize on what we know about intrinsic motivation: that is, they present interesting challenges and choices, are susceptible to alternative strategies and sustained effort, lead to a feeling of competence, and can be completed with others. Not all of these features can always be built into what happens in schools, but many can be, and in general, most schools and classrooms would be more interesting and energetic places if the attempt were made.

Apart from the design of classroom activities, which is explored in Chapter 8, "Designing Learning Experiences," there are important implications for the interactions among teachers and students, which are described briefly below.

Caring

For some students, depending on their circumstances, the nature of their relationships with individual teachers is life-transforming, providing much of the motivation for their commitment to school and even to a career. It's not unusual to hear successful professionals report that if it had not been for a particular teacher, someone who "really cared about me" or someone "who believed I could be somebody," they would never have pursued further education. The importance of these relationships is captured in the motto "They don't care what you know until they know that you care."

The deep caring that teachers express for their students may be reflected in many different styles. Some teachers are warm, with a friendly, joking approach. Others have a stern demeanor, projecting a tough exterior. But beneath all styles is an essential *caring,* an acceptance of the student as valued and worthy of support.

It should also be noted, however, that a caring teacher is not always a soft teacher; indeed, many are very strict. This attitude merely conveys high expectations, however. It is a way of saying, "If I didn't care about you, I would accept this paper as adequate. But I know you can do a much better job; please revise it and bring it back tomorrow." This confidence is not lost on students, who report, sometimes years later, that "She really made me want to do my best."

Praise

The research on motivation has important implications for teachers' use of praise. Of course, praise constitutes extrinsic motivation. Does this mean that it should never be used? Of course not, but its consequences must be clearly understood. Carol Dweck has shed a great deal of light on the nature of praise and how it can help and hinder students. She writes:

> After seven experiments with hundreds of children, we had some of the clearest findings I've ever seen: Praising children's intelligence harms their motivation and it harms their performance.
>
> How can that be? Don't children love to be praised? Yes, children love praise. And they especially love to be praised for their intelligence and their talent. It really does give them a boost, a special glow—but only for the moment. The minute they hit a snag, their confidence goes out the window and their motivation hits rock bottom. If success means they're smart, the failure means they're dumb. (2000, p. 170)

Dweck's point is that when students are praised for their intelligence, that praise undermines their resilience in the face of the inevitable difficulties that all learners experience. That is, when they depend on a teacher's (or parent's) praise for their feeling of worth, that praise substitutes for pride in work well done. Furthermore, it can undermine students' willingness to work hard. As Dweck says, "When we say to children: 'Wow, you did that so quickly!' or 'Look, you didn't make any mistakes!' what message are we sending? We are telling them that what we prize are speed and perfection. Speed and perfection are the enemy of difficult learning. . . ." (ibid., p. 173)

Does this mean that teachers should never praise students for their work? Not at all, but it does suggest that praise should be offered to students for their persistence, for the strategies used, for the insights they bring to their assignments. This approach tends to reinforce an attitude toward hard work that has been demonstrated to result in productive attitudes toward learning.

COMMENTARY ON THE INSTRUCTIONAL EXAMPLES

The instructional units described in the Appendix provide two illustrations of how the principles of student motivation may be applied in practice. These connections are applied below.

How Many Beans?

The question posed in this unit is very appealing to students; they are invited to estimate the number of beans in a jar. They then compare their estimates to those made by other groups of students who used different approaches.

As noted above, intellectual curiosity is an important motivator to all people, including young people. The question "How many beans are in a jar?" is virtually irresistible to students; many of them will begin by guessing wildly, not understanding at first that they are able to make a fairly close estimate of the answer. So, the question itself serves as a "hook" to draw students into an important exploration, one in which they apply computational skills to a practical situation and develop the important mathematical skill of estimation.

Furthermore, because students work in teams in this unit, they have the opportunity to connect with their classmates in answering an important question. In their groups they must listen to others' points of view, make a plan for proceeding, and determine who will be responsible for which aspect of the effort. The collaborative work is highly motivational, providing students with the forum for joint engagement with an interesting question.

The important element of choice is part of this unit as well; students select an approach to solving the problem from among those offered by the teacher (and supplemented, if necessary, by the teacher). Choice, even when exercised among a small number of options, gives students a sense of control over their lives and tends to bring forth greater effort, and more focused effort, than is possible when students are simply assigned a task.

Lastly, because students take on a challenging question and answer it in collaboration with classmates, they develop an important sense of efficacy and mastery. Initially, many students guess wildly about the number of beans in the jar; however, by the conclusion of the unit, students will appreciate the power of logical reasoning and will have arrived at a credible estimate. By explaining their thinking, students solidify their understanding of the process of mathematical reasoning and develop a firm grounding in the important skills involved. These skills may be applied to many other situations, and students are therefore in a position to tackle future reasoning problems with greater confidence. This sense of mastery is highly motivational and contributes to a sense of mastery and power.

Pre-Revolutionary America

This unit, in which students explore the many factors surrounding the signing of the Declaration of Independence, provides multiple paths to engaging students in important work. First, and in some respects most important, students themselves determine the question they would like to investigate. The importance of this element of choice cannot be overestimated.; it requires that students make a commitment to a question they find interesting and, along with a team of classmates, pursue it.

Naturally, by organizing the unit as a team exploration, the teacher permits students to do something that is very important to them, namely, connect with others. Teamwork, of course, carries certain risks; teachers must ensure that all students do their share of the work and that some students don't become "free riders" on the work of others. This may be an issue that should be addressed directly. But the advantages of group work are well documented; students tend to be more committed to a project when they risk letting others down. Furthermore, students are highly motivated to be in contact with one another and will pass notes if not permitted to talk. Group work serves the purpose of making interpersonal communication legitimate and, indeed, essential to achieving the purposes of the unit.

Over the course of the unit, as a consequence of both their own work and that of other teams, students develop insights into a critical period in American history and the motivations of those involved. This deep understanding, when solidified through group discussion and consolidated through the study guide and summative assessment, gives students an important sense of mastery and understanding. They don't just memorize historical facts and the names of persons; they come to *understand* the thinking and actions of the major players.

Summary

The research on student motivation confirms what many know from common sense: that when students care about what they are doing, they will devote incalculable energy to it. This energy is intrinsically driven; extrinsic rewards and punishments are very poor substitutes. These findings are profound and have implications for every aspect of classroom life, from the interaction of students and teachers to the organization of the classroom to the design of learning experiences. These topics are addressed in Parts 2 and 3 of this book.

Part 2

USING WHAT WE KNOW TO PROMOTE LEARNING

The most critical application of a teacher's knowledge and insight is to promote student learning. Educators know far more now than they did a generation ago about learning; teachers can use that knowledge in deciding exactly what they intend their students to learn, in promoting that learning, and in ensuring that their efforts have been successful.

In the current environment of top-down accountability demands, it's easy to lose sight of the fact that teachers exercise enormous discretion in their work. Even in the context of state and national curriculum standards, teachers must still decide, on a daily and hourly basis, what to teach their students. These decisions are largely based, of course, on the school's or district's established curriculum, but they are also strongly affected by teachers' knowledge of their own students and what they need to learn next.

The first obligation, then, of teachers is to know their students as well as possible so that they can make appropriate decisions concerning content and methodology. Naturally, teachers' responsibilities affect the depth of this knowledge; a kindergarten teacher with 17 students can know each of them far better than can a high school teacher with 150. Then, with the demands of the curriculum in mind, teachers determine which learning outcomes to emphasize on any given day and how they will know whether students have actually learned what they intended. Not just any assessment will do; teachers must choose, from the full range of possibilities, a method of assessment that is suitable to the learning they intend and that will help steer both them and their students toward complete understanding.

Lastly, teachers must determine how to promote student learning of important content. This is where teachers' understanding of the active nature of learning and the individuality of students bears the greatest fruit. With this knowledge, teachers can create learning experiences in which students are intellectually active and take responsibility for their own learning. Such instructional design constitutes the heart of teaching; here teachers exhibit their greatest creativity and professionalism.

Part 2 encompasses all these issues: providing guidance for teachers in using what they know about content, assessment, learning, and motivation to promote high-level learning among their students.

Chapter 5

Knowing Our Students

Classes are filled with students, and although it is essential to understand, in theoretical terms, how people learn and how they are motivated to expend their best efforts in the service of learning, it is the individual students with whom teachers must, in the end, connect.

INTRODUCTION

In order for teachers to ensure student learning, they must, of course, know in depth the subjects they teach. There is no shortcut for this; it's not sufficient to be a page or two ahead of the class. Without a deep understanding of content, a teacher can't design meaningful learning activities or formulate good questions around which to structure a lesson. Indeed, the teacher can't even recognize an important question when it comes from a student or distinguish an important question from a trivial one. Thus, content knowledge is essential for effective teaching.

However, important as content knowledge is, it is not sufficient. A teacher does not present knowledge in a vacuum; he or she introduces it *to students*. It's not enough to make a brilliant presentation. In order to understand content, students must be *engaged* with it, and in order to create such engagement, teachers must understand their students. They must understand the context in which their students are participating in the enterprise called school; they can do this only if they understand their students as individuals and as members of larger cultural communities.

Naturally, teachers' opportunities for developing a deep understanding of their students vary according to their situations and their teaching assignments. A kindergarten teacher with 19 students knows more about each of them than a high school band teacher who interacts with 400 students each week. But the principle is the same: Teachers teach *students*, and they must be aware of those students' worlds.

Understanding one's students has many different aspects, ranging from developmental characteristics, to their cultural and home environments, to their stage of learning and interests. Teachers sensitive to their students are aware of all these factors when they design learning experiences; they recognize that a student's experience in school is filtered through all these factors and cannot be considered independently of them. There are many sources of individual differences among children. For this reason, it's not possible to think about a "typical" class of third graders or high school juniors. There is simply too much variation.

HOME SITUATION

Many students have relatively uncomplicated home situations: There is sufficient food on the table, one or both parents have jobs paying well enough to sustain a reasonable lifestyle, and other members of the family are healthy. But some students endure, daily, conditions that seriously compromise their capacity to make the most of opportunities at school. They may not know where they will sleep that night or their home may consist of the back seat of a car. Even if they are not homeless, their family's income may only be sufficient to permit very crowded living conditions, with no quiet, private place to which children may retreat or complete schoolwork. Or they may move frequently, staying a few days ahead of the date when rent payments are due. Students may need to prepare the evening meal for younger siblings or play an important role in getting them off to school in the morning. When siblings are sick, their older sister or brother may be obliged to stay home from school to care for them.

Alternatively, students may live in environments of high emotional stress, with serious physical or emotional illness having struck a parent or sibling. Such stress can greatly reduce a student's capacity to concentrate in class, to complete assignments, and to make a commitment to schoolwork. The serious illness or death of a parent creates fear of abandonment (what will become of me?); that of a sibling often results in a feeling of guilt (why not me?). In either situation, students' capacity for high-level intellectual work is seriously compromised.

Other, less dramatic home situations can also have an impact on students' ability to engage seriously in school. The normal stresses of growing up—sibling rivalry, adolescent angst, and parental conflicts—may consume energy that, in a more favorable environment, could be devoted to schoolwork.

In order to teach students effectively, it's important for teachers to know as much as possible about their home environments. Students themselves are frequently an important source of this information; young children, in particular, are keen to describe their families, the interests they share with their siblings, and how they spend their time on weekends. This information must, of course, be volunteered by students, but when it is, it can provide teachers with important insights into their lives.

In some schools, teachers conduct home visits, particularly to the homes of very young children. Although this practice is rare, it's difficult not to appreciate its value. All teachers, however, have the opportunity to meet the families of the children they teach during formally structured open houses, back-to-school nights, or parent-teacher conferences. If parents are never able to attend such events, this may signal an unstable environment, which could cause teachers concern.

Teachers occasionally become aware of aspects of a student's home environment that are alarming and deserve more careful scrutiny. Every state sponsors programs to protect children from abuse, and sometimes a teacher is the person best positioned to notice symptoms of a child's distress. Such situations should be referred to other specialists in the school, such as a social worker, a counselor, or the school's principal.

CULTURAL ENVIRONMENT

Throughout its history, the United States has been a melting pot of immigrants from around the world; an important source of its appeal for potential immigrants has been the perceived opportunity for advancement based on merit, without regard to family connections or social status. This goal has not, of course, been fully realized: Many immigrants, even when they enter the country legally, find themselves trapped in low-wage jobs with little potential to move up. However, the goal has always been part of the "American dream" and has resulted in the desire of many recent arrivals to the United States to assimilate rapidly into American society.

The melting pot image of the United States still prevails, and in recent years the nation has attracted record numbers of immigrants. But the patterns have shifted; even those parts of the country (such as the upper Midwest) that formerly had extremely homogeneous populations now attract new arrivals from Southeast Asia, Latin America, or the Indian subcontinent.

It is not unusual for over 50 languages to be spoken in the homes of students of a mid-sized school anywhere in the United States.

Such language diversity presents enormous instructional challenges as teachers strive to help students learn to read and to understand a variety of subjects in a language other than their native tongue. But there are cultural implications as well. In some cultures, it is disrespectful to challenge authority or to look an adult in the eye. Such cultural patterns may affect how students interpret classroom interactions or may inhibit them from questioning, for example, a textbook's account of an historical event. Furthermore, in some cultures, children are raised by the entire community, with the extended family playing an important role. Thus, it may not be sufficient for a teacher to establish contact with a student's parents, since grandparents or aunts and uncles may contribute materially to that student's upbringing. Cultural differences may also cause some students to feel isolated from the mainstream or to stay with others from their own language or cultural group. Regardless of the manner in which cultural factors play out in the classroom, teachers must be aware of the backgrounds of their students in order to interact sensitively with them and their families.

Teachers have multiple opportunities to learn about their students' cultures, beginning with asking them to describe their background, either individually or as part of a group activity. Most students are proud of their cultural heritage, particularly when it is received by a teacher and classmates with interest and respect. Many teachers, as part of their cultural studies, ask students to interview older members of their community on such topics as how they lived as children, the stories that were handed down, and the like. Such conversations can be rich and will cause all students to feel welcome in the classroom.

LEVEL OF COGNITIVE DEVELOPMENT

The patterns of cognitive development are universal and follow well-researched routes as children mature through adolescence. However, within those universal patterns are considerable individual differences that help to explain the wide variation within a class. Some children entering kindergarten have a solid concept of number. Others do not yet use numbers with confidence; they are not sure, for example, that seven objects are the same quantity if they are spread out. A grasp of proportional reasoning is essential for understanding algebra, yet many middle school students have not yet attained it.

Teachers find that understanding their students' levels of cognitive development is an extremely interesting and valuable aspect of knowing them, enabling them to create appropriate learning experiences. Many simple techniques may be used, which vary, naturally, with the age of the children. For example, a teacher can check for students' understanding of the stability of length by holding two pencils up parallel to one another and establishing with the students (of first or second grade) that they are the same length. If the teacher then moves one of the pencils so that their end points are no longer lined up, some students will believe that one pencil is now longer than the other. Until the concept of length is established solidly in children's minds, their capacity to measure accurately will be seriously compromised.

Other such examples abound, addressing the stability of the concept of number, weight, volume, and mass, as well as the skills of proportional reasoning and combinatorial logic. These concepts are prerequisite for understanding much of the curriculum in mathematics and science. Until these concepts are understood, students will not be in a position to understand those subjects. Thus, an important aspect of teachers' responsibility is to ascertain the students' levels of cognitive development and to make the necessary adjustments in their instruction.

SKILLS AND KNOWLEDGE

Every class contains students with a wide range of skills and knowledge. Some children enter kindergarten with a vocabulary of 3,000 words; others can barely express themselves. Family environment is, of course, an important factor contributing to children's initial level of skill. In some language-rich households, parents read regularly to their children. They also provide enriching experiences, such as regularly taking them to parks and on other excursions.

But in school children progress at very different rates, as any teacher can attest. In fact, the range of knowledge and skills displayed by children entering kindergarten increases as they grow older. Thus, in a typical class of third graders, some students read with ease, whereas others still struggle to decode; some think in abstract terms about mathematical concepts, whereas others work concretely. These differences are normal, but they have enormous implications for a teacher's planning and execution of learning experiences. Some of these differences are developmental, of course, as described in the previous section. But others are simply a reflection of the progress made by different students in the school's curriculum.

Furthermore, many classes include students with special needs, increasing the requirement for teachers to be sensitive to individual differences. Special education is an important specialty in its own right, and many special-needs students will have additional support when they are mainstreamed into a regular classroom; such support takes the form of an aide or special materials. But even when they have such support, it's important for all teachers to be sensitive to how life appears to students with special needs so that they can make adjustments where possible and ensure that such students are fully accepted by the other students in the class.

A teacher's primary source of information about students' skills and knowledge is the students themselves: the questions they ask in class, their performance on written work, and their responses to classroom activities. Of course, cumulative folders and prior teachers may be valuable sources of information, but teachers need to be wary of the possible distortions resulting from the perspectives of others.

INTERESTS AND EXPERIENCES

Individual students have their own talents and interests. One student may be highly artistic; another may be a whiz at numbers. Some students find an important source of pride in athletic prowess, others in music. These interests may have a direct bearing on school learning or may be independent of it. But either way, it's important for teachers, to the extent possible, to be aware of their students' strengths and interests. The educational literature is filled with inspiring examples of teachers who were able to connect with individual students when they asked them to draw on an area of special interest and experience in developing, for example, their skill in writing or in creating mathematics problems involving an operation such as multiplication. One example concerns a high school sophomore who was alienated from school and refused to be involved in the events of English class. But when his teacher expressed interest in basketball, this student's passion outside of school hours, he found that he could, through his writing, "teach" his teacher the nuances of the game. The student was an expert on the subject, and it provided a vehicle for written expression highly valued by both the student and the teacher.

In addition, students have had numerous experiences, both in school and beyond, and accomplished teachers are skilled in relating these experiences to school learning. Some experiences are virtually universal; for example, most students are aware of the behavior of a ball when it is thrown from a person's hand. Teachers can build on this knowledge when explaining the concept of gravitational force. Other experiences are more individualized: When students interview their grandparents about conditions 50 years ago, the stories they hear will be unique to their grandparents' situations. If students have traveled widely, or if they have moved from another town, state, or country, they will arrive with experiences all their own.

One of the fundamental truths of learning is that students build on their past experiences when learning new concepts; when introducing students to new ideas, accomplished teachers take care to relate those concepts to experiences the students bring with them or have acquired in school. But teachers cannot relate their lessons to students' experiences if they are not aware of them. Thus, accomplished teachers invest considerable energy in learning about their students, including their important experiences that can relate to what they will be learning in class. Techniques used by teachers for learning about their students' interests and skills include conversation, conducting interest inventories, and attending, when they can, activities in which their students are involved, such as athletic or musical events. The benefits of taking a personal interest in their students extend well beyond learning about them for the purpose of planning learning experiences; such interest also pays enormous dividends in the relationships teachers can create with their students—relationships of interest and concern.

ATTITUDES TOWARD SCHOOL

When they enter kindergarten, all children are eager to begin school. It is symbolic of growing up, which is irresistible to young children. Kindergarten, or first grade if kindergarten is not available to them, is where they begin a new stage of their life, and for virtually all children this is an important step. In some cultures, for example in Japan, beginning school is marked by numerous rituals, which only adds to its significance. Children are provided a book bag and some simple supplies; these items indicate to children that they are now students and that the work they do in school should represent serious effort.

Of course, for some children, beginning school, and its accompanying separation from a parent, can be a wrenching experience. However, even children who find the initial steps difficult adjust quickly to the new setting and set about exploring the environment, making friends, and discovering what can be done with materials in the classroom.

However, although virtually all children are eager to enter school, not all of them remain keen. It is rare to encounter an intellectually lazy 5-year-old but, unfortunately, there are many intellectually lethargic 14-year-olds. It is well recognized that in many (typically middle and high) schools, there is a belief, at least among some students, that it's not "cool" to be smart, to work hard, to try to excel, to care (or to be seen to care).

Such attitudes among students present an enormous challenge for teachers, and they may need to be addressed directly. From the point of view of knowing one's students, it's important to recognize that this cluster of attitudes—of not caring, of not being willing to commit to hard work—may be a serious factor that must be addressed in the design of learning experiences and in one's interaction with students and their families. Fortunately, the same principles of lesson and unit design that yield high-quality student learning also serve to undermine the negative attitudes toward school held by some students. However, it remains the case that with some students, and with some groups of students, overcoming negative attitudes toward school can be a serious endeavor.

Summary

Knowing one's students is a fundamental responsibility of teaching; as teachers become more experienced, their techniques become both more extensive and streamlined. They know, for example, how to learn as much as possible simply by overhearing students' discussions or engaging them in informal conversation. They become skilled at talking with parents and other caregivers to elicit important aspects of a student's home life or interests beyond school. They become adept at observing students in class to determine their level of skill in the school's curriculum and the level of development of their cognitive structures. This information is enormously valuable to teachers as they design learning experiences, ensuring that those experiences are appropriate to all students.

Chapter 6

Establishing Learning Outcomes

OVERVIEW

On any given day or in any given hour, the first and arguably the most important questions a teacher must be able to answer are "What do I want my students to learn? When they leave here at the end of the day or the week, what will they know, or what will they be able to do, that they don't know or can't do now?" This is not the same as what the students will do or what the teacher will do—it refers to what the students will *learn*. Thus, the answer to the question about intended learning is not that the students will "do page 46" or will "read Chapter Four and answer the questions at the end." That is, when asked about his or her plans, a teacher thinking in terms of student learning would not reply that they are "doing *Hamlet*" or "factoring polynomials."

Instead, a teacher would report that in studying *Hamlet,* the students will understand the structure of the plot, or the essential characteristics of a dramatic tragedy, or the techniques used by an author to reveal character traits. Alternatively, in the study of factoring polynomials, the teacher would specify that students will be able to recognize the different patterns involved in polynomials (for example, the difference of squares) and how to solve them efficiently. Therefore, learning outcomes are different from learning activities; activities refer to what students will *do,* whereas learning outcomes refer to what they will *learn*. Teaching, in other words, is a purposeful, goal-directed activity. The activities in which students engage *result* in the desired learning, but they are not the learning itself.

Clarity in understanding learning outcomes is absolutely essential for instructional planning. Many teachers are skilled at designing engaging activities for students, but if these are not in the service of a learning purpose, they are, in effect, merely "fun and games." This is not to suggest that engagement in learning is never fun (indeed, it should be, in the sense of being an intellectual challenge), only that it should never be *merely* fun. For teachers new to the profession, this can be a difficult distinction; the teacher is only one person, after all, and the students are numerous; keeping them productively occupied is, understandably, a teacher's highest priority. But behind the engagement lies the purpose of the engagement—the intended learning, the outcomes.

TERMINOLOGY

Many different terms are used by both practitioners and policymakers to refer to the results of schooling: *content and performance standards, outcomes, goals, objectives, expectations, benchmarks,* and others. The precise meaning of these terms is frequently not specified; educators either blur the meanings or, what may be worse, create artificial distinctions among them. Thus, clarity is important, and it's helpful to establish terminology that people can agree to use.

Standards, outcomes, and *goals* tend to refer to the large aims of student learning; standards are typically mandated by state agencies and are reflected in large-scale state tests. *Outcomes* and *goals* are terms used more frequently by educators at the school and district levels. *Benchmarks* refer generally to the expected learning at different stages of schooling—for example, third-grade or eighth-grade benchmarks. *Objectives,* on the other hand, usually refer to the intended learning as the result of a single lesson's activities.

What's important in deciding on terminology is to be clear. It's essential that everyone know what one is referring to when one uses terms like *goals* or *outcomes*. And when educators, policymakers, or vendors claim that something is *standards-based,* what do they actually mean? Consensus on terminology is important, not because any particular terminology is correct but so that educators can communicate with one another and with members of the public. The term used in this book to describe intended student learning is *outcomes.* This term is used to refer to the desired results of student learning at any level of detail: There can be program outcomes as well as unit or lesson outcomes.

LEVEL OF DETAIL

Teachers must think about what they want their students to learn at a number of different levels of detail simultaneously, and these levels are nested within one another. Teachers must think about today: "What do I intend my students to have learned or become aware of by the end of today's lesson?" But today's lesson is embedded in the week's or unit's study of the topic: a unit on, for example, the pre-Revolutionary period of U.S. history or an investigation of unlike fractions. And those outcomes, in turn, contribute to student learning during the entire year of studying history or mathematics, all of which should support the goals the school has developed for the course and the state's content standards.

A program—for example, that of a high school mathematics department—will have broad outcomes toward which it directs students in all its courses, including such things as computational skill, algebraic manipulation, pattern recognition, problem solving and application, and so on. All courses in the department—for example, algebra, geometry, trigonometry, differential calculus, and business math—advance this range of outcomes as appropriate to their particular content. Similarly, program goals for the social studies department might include both content (facts and trends in world history, U.S. history, institutions of government, economics, and geography) and skills (map reading, pattern recognition, political argument, and historical analysis). These program goals are then addressed in each of the courses offered in the department.

The different levels of detail (or grain size), in ascending level of generality, are as follows:

> ***Lesson outcomes.***   For every lesson, teachers must know what they intend students to learn. This intended learning provides the structure for the learning experiences in which students are engaged and for which the teacher is alert for evidence of student mastery. The lesson outcomes may be the same for every member of the class, but they may also be customized to fit the situation of subgroups (or even individuals) within the class.
>
> Such modification of lesson outcomes (called *differentiation* in the educational literature) is the mark of a truly experienced and accomplished teacher. It requires knowing, in considerable detail, where each student "is" in his or her learning and therefore recognizing what would represent an appropriate challenge. And, of course, modification has implications for the design of instructional activities; ideally, the same task will offer multiple challenges simultaneously, but this is not always possible. This matter will be addressed more fully in Chapter 8, "Designing Learning Experiences."
>
> ***Unit outcomes.***   A unit consists of a series of lessons devoted to a single topic or to a broad understanding. For example, a unit in high school English might be devoted to studying *Hamlet* or one in fourth-grade mathematics to the skills of estimation of large

numbers. Whereas detailed planning occurs at the lesson level, unit planning provides the essential road map for planning and for the design of summative assessments (see Chapter 7, "Assessing Student Learning").

In most curricula, units are stated in terms of their topics, with their outcomes then articulated in detail. One can read the list of topics and derive a sense of the course, that is, its general direction. But until one reads the unit outcomes, and indeed, until one sees the actual assessments to be used, it's not possible to know the specific learning intended by the teacher.

Course outcomes. A course consists of the anticipated learning for an entire year in a discipline, whether it is freshman English or fourth-grade mathematics. These outcomes are typically organized according to the *strands* of the discipline rather than simply as an addition of the unit outcomes. For example, a course in fifth-grade language arts will contain outcomes in reading, writing, speaking, listening, and viewing. A course in seventh-grade mathematics will include outcomes in number and numerical operations, geometry and measurement, patterns and algebra, data analysis and probability, and mathematical processes. These strands typically represent the principal categories of learning in each discipline and are developed, as appropriate, at each level of schooling. Teachers sometimes—particularly if they are the only teacher in a school teaching a course, such as trigonometry, or the only teacher at a grade level in an elementary school—will take the responsibility for writing course outcomes. More typically, however, such outcomes (and their accompanying tests or exams) are prepared by teachers working together in their departments or grade levels.

Program outcomes. At the highest level of generality are program outcomes, the broad statements of learning, typically within the strands described above, for each discipline. For example, a school's or district's program in language arts might have as one of its program outcomes that "students will demonstrate effective skill in writing for a variety of audiences and purposes." The program outcomes in science might include the statement that students can "design and execute experiments in life, physical, and earth sciences." In general, individual teachers don't write program outcomes; these are typically written (or adopted from national organizations) by districtwide curriculum committees.

SOURCES OF LEARNING OUTCOMES

Teachers, in their work with students, must be able to state, in clear terms, what their outcomes are for student learning. Even in states and districts with a unified curriculum, teachers, when they close their doors to work with their students, are in charge of their world. In practical terms, individual teachers have considerable authority over what they do with their students. Even when there is a mandated curriculum, teachers can always go beyond the established syllabus when determining what they want their students to learn.

In deciding, then, what they want their students to learn, on a given day or in a given unit, what are the influences affecting a teacher's choice? On what do such decisions depend?

State curriculum frameworks. State curriculum frameworks provide a structure for most learning outcomes; depending on the specificity with which they are written, they may offer anywhere from general guidance to detailed requirements. At the very least, the learning outcomes a teacher establishes for a lesson or a unit must be consistent with those identified in a state curriculum framework.

Thus, New Jersey's social studies core curriculum standards include one for U.S. and N.J. history that states: "All students will demonstrate knowledge of United States and New Jersey history in order to understand life and events in the past and how they relate to the present and future." One of the standards in mathematics states that "all students will represent and analyze relationships among variable quantities and solve problems involving patterns, functions, and algebraic concepts and processes."

Such statements are very broad, providing only the most general map of the complex terrain of the discipline. And although most states require that schools align their own programs and courses with the state's curriculum standards, the generality of the statements offers little true guidance. Their real meaning, therefore, at both the program and course levels, appears in their assessments. Similarly, because they are so broad, they may be used to justify virtually any content that a school or an individual teacher chooses to include in a course.

District/school curricula.   Some schools and districts specify in great detail the content of every course or grade level and discipline. Others adopt an externally developed *program* or textbook series that does the same thing, sometimes going so far as to supply a *script* for the teacher to say. If teachers are handed a "teacher-proof" curriculum, then, they have little choice but to teach it as written.

However, such situations are rare; more typically, teachers are asked to teach a course with established final outcomes or a common final assessment for which they are required to prepare their students. Within that structure they have considerable flexibility in terms of how they organize the course, what units of study they develop, and what daily learning outcomes and activities they devise.

Structure of the discipline.   In selecting what they want their students to learn, teachers must be aware of the important concepts and skills in the discipline and how they are related to one another. It's essential that any learning outcomes for students represent important learning. It is not sufficient that a certain concept be easy or fun for teachers to teach or for students to learn; it should also be important for them to learn.

An important aspect of the structure of a discipline relates to prerequisite relationships within the discipline; these are more important in some disciplines than in others. For example, students can't understand addition or subtraction with regrouping until their understanding of place value is secure. They can, of course, memorize a procedure to get the right answer, but if they don't understand the underlying concept of place value, this procedural knowledge is superficial and students can't solve problems that deviate from the specific models they have learned. Similarly, proficiency in a second language depends on carefully constructed building blocks of vocabulary and linguistic structure; the present tense of verbs must typically be mastered before students move on to the past or future tenses, to say nothing of the conditional or the subjunctive mood or the distinction between the active and passive voice.

Different types of outcomes.   As described in Chapter 1, "What We Know About Content," learning outcomes may be of several different types: knowledge (factual, procedural, conceptual), skills (thinking and reasoning, communication, and social), and values and dispositions. Any lesson or unit will include outcomes of most of these different types; indeed, a teacher's creativity in weaving multiple purposes into a unit is a mark of both experience and expertise. For example, a fifth-grade science unit in buoyancy will include outcomes related to factual knowledge and conceptual understanding (what is buoyancy, and how is it related to floating?), thinking skills (such as making predictions about what will happen if a given object is placed in water or in another liquid, or separating and controlling variables in designing an experiment to find the answer), communication skills (such as describing one's findings about buoyancy and displacement in writing or in an oral presentation), and collaboration skills (such as working productively with classmates).

The opportunity to develop collaborative skills is one reason teachers use instructional strategies such as cooperative learning in their classes. The skills of group work—active listening, respecting others' views, dividing work fairly and assigning roles, planning work and monitoring its completion, and assisting others—can be actively taught and then incorporated into daily classroom activities.

COORDINATION AND INTEGRATION

As stated above, teachers are obliged to be clear—to their colleagues, their administrators, and their students and parents—about what their intended learning outcomes are for students in any given lesson or in the unit containing that lesson. Furthermore, because a state's curriculum standards are listed individually, it is tempting to think that one must, as a teacher, address them separately. However, this is definitely not the case. By addressing many outcomes simultaneously within a single lesson or unit, teachers can enrich the opportunities they provide for students.

Coordination refers to the practice of addressing topics from different disciplines at the same time so as to make their connections visible. This is possible even if students are enrolled in separate courses at the high school level; their teachers have engaged in joint planning, so they address related topics simultaneously. A dramatic illustration of this practice is in coordinating topics in history and literature: For example, high school juniors frequently study American literature and U.S. history simultaneously. The literature is placed in a historical context and, at the same time, provides a window on the historical period. In addition, the literature provides a valuable social window on the historical period. Neither of these perspectives is possible without such coordination. Even when history and literature are taught in different departments, as in a high school, the coordination of topics enriches both classes.

Integration refers to the practice of embedding the skills and knowledge of one discipline in another discipline so that they constitute, from the students' perspective, a seamless whole. For example, when students are asked to write about their findings from an investigation in science, they not only consolidate their understanding of the science, they also improve their skills in expository writing. Similarly, skills of data analysis may be taught or reinforced in both science (finding the mean or median from a data set) and social studies (discerning trends across a historical period).

Teachers of elementary students have the greatest opportunities to engage in both coordination and integration of curriculum topics and outcomes, because they work with their students virtually all day and are responsible for the entire curriculum. Such coordination and integration are also possible at the high school level, although they require coordination not only of the curriculum outcomes, but of the teachers' schedules as well. For most teachers such pooling of effort requires some time to arrange, but it is time that is very well spent.

Some instructional teams (typically at the elementary level) select a theme (such as "rivers") for the year and organize much of their program around it. In these cases, the students read literature inspired by rivers, explore ancient and modern civilizations settled on rivers, and engage in mathematical and scientific explorations within the context of rivers. Naturally, the students study other topics as well, but the choice of a single large theme unifies the curriculum in a way not possible otherwise.

OTHER ISSUES

There are several additional issues related to curriculum outcomes, which are under the control of teachers. These are addressed below.

Public versus Private Outcomes

An issue regarding curriculum outcomes relates to their public or private nature. The question is "Should the curriculum outcomes be known, and if so, by whom?"

There can be little argument that curriculum outcomes at all levels should be public and transparent to the professional community; indeed, in most places this is required. It is also essential that they be made known to the parents of one's students, particularly the parents of elementary school students, who tend to take a keen interest in their children's education. Many schools post their learning outcomes, at least the program and course outcomes, on their Web sites for anyone to peruse.

The issue makes sense only when applied to students: "Should I, as a teacher, tell my students what my learning outcomes are for a day's lesson? Should I write the objectives on the board? Should I announce them at the beginning of the lesson?"

There are two schools of thought here, and the proper course of action involves striking a balance. It's important for students to know, in general, what they are going to learn and why. And as students grow older, this awareness becomes more critical. Some teachers make a point of declaring, at the beginning of each day's lesson, what the students will be learning that day and where it fits into the larger scheme of the instructional program.

There are times, however, when such announcements are unnecessary and may even undermine students' learning. When students are engaged in a scientific inquiry—for example, dealing with the concept of buoyancy—what is important, at least initially, is for them to understand what they are to *do;* the learning will emerge in the course of the lesson or possibly over the course of several lessons. That is, students must be clear about their task: "Can you make this lump of clay float? And after you've found a way to make it float (creating, in effect, a boat shape), can you make a *good* boat, that is, one that can hold a large number of paper clips?" Naturally, teachers must be clear about their learning outcomes at all times, even when they have not yet revealed them to the students. But in promoting learning, it's not essential for the students to be informed at the outset of the teacher's longer-range purposes.

Of course, when teachers have led students through a series of learning experiences organized around an important concept, such as buoyancy, they must bring the series to closure and help students consolidate their understanding. Although students may have conducted a series of investigations and learned, for example, that the amount of water displaced by a vessel is related to its volume, not its weight, they need to understand why this is the case. Hence, as part of bringing the unit to closure, the teacher will invite students to share their learning and will relate one finding to another, drawing out the general principles. Such opportunities for reflection and closure are at the heart of expert teaching.

Consistency

Another issue is, to what extent should different teachers, in the same school and teaching the same subject, establish the same learning outcomes for their students? Further, should teachers of the same course, for example Algebra I, work from the same course outline, even if they teach in different schools but within a single district?

In general, the answer is "yes." Teachers must be able to assure the teachers who will receive their students in subsequent years that those students are adequately prepared to succeed in the next course. For example, other math teachers must know that any students who have taken Algebra I in the school or the district have mastered certain knowledge and skills. In practice, this requirement for consistency is manifested in the practice of teachers working together to develop a common end-of-course assessment, which they all administer.

Naturally, if a teacher is the sole teacher of an elective course, primarily at the high school level, that teacher has complete discretion as to the content of the course so long as it fits within the state's curriculum framework. This is particularly the case if the subject of the course, for example psychology, is one in which the state has not developed content standards. But as a general rule, consistency within a school and across a school district is important; it is through the curriculum outcomes (and the accompanying assessments) that a course's content is established. The title "Freshman English" should have a common meaning to everyone who uses it. Teachers will have their own specialties, of course, and will choose to put their own stamp on a course. However, everyone should know, within the English department and across the district, what students learn in English when they are ninth graders.

COMMENTARY ON THE INSTRUCTIONAL EXAMPLES

The instructional examples used in this book illustrate the principles of curriculum design in several important ways, both in emphasizing important learning and in citing instructional outcomes from several different categories.

How Many Beans?

This unit engages elementary students in estimating the number of beans in a jar. Its outcomes include the essential skills of estimating and of thinking through a multistep process. It also enables students to apply their skills in computation to a practical situation, thereby illustrating the importance and relevance of these skills.

The curriculum outcomes in "How Many Beans?" include procedural knowledge, reasoning, communication and collaboration skills, and aesthetics. The problem itself is easily conceptualized ("How many beans are in this jar?"), yet the variety of solutions to the problem illustrates the complexity of even simple mathematical questions.

The exploration engages different groups of students in finding different methods of solution, emphasizing an important aspect of mathematical reasoning, namely, that there is frequently more than one approach to a problem. Examining the different methods enables students to compare them for both accuracy (how close they are to the actual number) and elegance of the approach. Mathematical elegance is an important aesthetic idea, one valued by mathematicians but rarely introduced to students; this unit offers a rare opportunity to illustrate it to elementary students.

This brief unit provides an approach to integration of curriculum outcomes across several disciplines. It is primarily situated in elementary mathematics, but because students must produce both an oral and a written explanation of their work, it provides an opportunity to incorporate communication skills into the mathematics curriculum. If an aerial photograph of a demonstration is used for the test for this unit, such a photograph could provide an opportunity to explore the concepts of demonstrations and free speech, a clear connection with the study of politics and government.

Pre-Revolutionary America

In this unit, high school students conduct an investigation on a question of their own creation regarding the run-up to the signing of the Declaration of Independence. This offers an opportunity for them to acquire both factual knowledge and conceptual understanding, use deep reasoning skills in their analysis of information, and collaborate with classmates. In the course of the unit they also communicate their findings both orally and in writing, further developing several aspects of communication skills.

This unit offers students the opportunity to "do history" in the sense that the unit reflects the structure of historical understanding. In the 21st century, of course, we know how the struggle between the American colonies and the English government was resolved; the colonists won their independence. However, for those living at the time, the outcome was unknown and unknowable. Furthermore, the colonists who signed the Declaration of Independence were committing a treasonable act; although their action now has the feeling of inevitability, it was actually highly risky. This unit captures some of the uncertain nature of the conflict of the time, enabling students to enter into the 18th-century context.

This unit is particularly appropriate for adolescent students in that it stretches their thinking about historical events. It invites them to think not only about the established facts of what occurred, but also about ethical considerations related to the period: How similar was the thinking of residents in the different colonies with respect to their relationship with England? Why would some colonists have preferred to remain part of the British Empire? How widespread was the phenomenon of different attitudes toward independence dividing families? Who was right in an ethical sense? Why do you think so?

Some of the teacher's outcomes for this unit are traditional in nature: Students will acquire information about the pre-Revolutionary period; they will know the facts of what occurred, the names of the people involved, and the dates of important events. Further, they will develop an understanding of the relationships among many of the individuals (Which ones were related to one another and how?) and of what was at stake for them in the impending crisis (What were they risking? Would they have lost property? Could they have lost their lives?).

Other teacher outcomes for the unit are less traditional, because the unit provides an opportunity for students to strengthen their skills of information gathering and data analysis. And because they are asked to work in teams, the unit gives students the chance to further develop their skills in collaborative inquiry.

It should be noted that the teacher must exercise skill in shaping students' investigations in such a manner that the desired outcomes will be achieved. Students may initially express interest in exploring a question that the experienced teacher knows represents a dead end of some sort. Perhaps information on the topic is very hard to acquire, or the answer to the question is trivial, or the entire area of inquiry is not central to the colonial struggle. The teacher's response in these cases is important to calibrate; it's important not to veto a student's question but rather to shape it, through questions and suggestions, as one that is more likely to yield important findings.

Summary

The establishment of clear student learning outcomes at all levels (daily lesson, unit, and course) is essential for good instructional planning; such outcomes cast a very long shadow over every other aspect of planning: learning activities, grouping of students, instructional materials, and assessment design. Once teachers knows what they intend students to learn, they can engage in the rest of instructional planning. Of course, as they acquire experience, teachers will be able to design their lessons with increasing ease, without extensive written plans for each step of the process. But regardless of their level of experience, accomplished teachers are always exceedingly clear about their intended outcomes.

Samples of learning outcomes for two units are provided in Appendix: Instructional Examples.

Chapter 7

Assessing Student Learning

Although essential, it is not sufficient to be clear about what students are to learn (the learning outcomes); it is also necessary to determine how to know that they *have* learned it and how to use assessment as part of the instructional process. Teachers must be clear in their own minds, and must be able to explain clearly to others, what their plan is for assessing student learning. They may develop this plan individually or with colleagues, but regardless of the source, it must be a *plan*.

In practice, identifying learning outcomes and their assessments are opposite sides of the same coin. That is, the *definition* of the learning outcomes consists of the assessments of those outcomes. For example, when the curriculum states that "Students will solve two-step word problems," and one inquires what that means, the response is that "Students could solve problems like the following. . . ." Thus, the assessments themselves become the operational definition of the outcomes; it is only through well-designed, appropriate assessments that a teacher can answer the following questions: "How do I know that my students have learned what I intended?" "What has not yet been learned satisfactorily?" "If students don't understand the concept(s) I intend them to learn, why not? What misconceptions do they hold? Where are the 'holes' in their understanding?"

As noted in Chapter 2, "What We Know About Assessment," there are two fundamental types of assessment: summative (determining the extent to which students have mastered the curriculum) and formative (using assessment to guide learning). When teachers give a test, for example, with the results of the test contributing to students' grades, they are conducting a summative assessment; when they give a quiz that students go over in class, or when they circulate while students are working and provide feedback on their work, they are engaging in formative assessment. Teachers use both types of assessment and must have the skills to use them well.

SUMMATIVE ASSESSMENTS

Either on their own or in collaboration with colleagues, teachers create summative assessments of student learning to determine the extent to which students understand what they have been learning. These take many forms: tests, projects, papers, presentations, and the like. In using what we know about assessment, educators must not only consider what the right approach is; they must also understand what is wrong about much that was done in the past.

The Limitations of Traditional Practice

A feature of many nightmares is the helpless feeling of arriving to take an exam and feeling completely unprepared. Even when they believe themselves prepared, test taking is, for many, fraught with anxiety. Many adults still recall the sweaty palms and nervous stomach that accompanied their encounter with the test paper or the "blue book." And most people have had the experience of studying the wrong thing, of not being asked on the test anything for which they had prepared. Or, worse, the test seemed to be devised purely to catch students with trick questions on obscure items that were not central to the manner in which the teacher presented the material or what students were asked to do. As Tom Guskey (2003) has pointed out, what students learn from practices such as tests that include items that were barely mentioned in class, or trick questions, is that "hard work and effort don't pay off in school because the time and effort they spent studying had little or no influence on the results . . . and . . . they cannot trust their teachers" (p. 8).

Rather than tests as guessing games, in which students try to read the teacher's mind, classroom assessments should provide students the opportunity to show what they have learned. There should be no surprises, particularly when students take the work seriously and exert their best effort. But some have misgivings when teachers tell students what is important for them to learn, direct their instructional efforts to those ends, and then prepare an assessment reflecting those same purposes. Is this not teaching to the test? And is there not something unethical about that?

The short answer is "no"; there is nothing unethical about this practice. After all, the teacher has only (1) been clear about the desired outcomes of instruction, (2) offered instruction to achieve those outcomes, and then (3) assessed students' performance to ensure that they have indeed achieved those outcomes. To do otherwise, to teach one thing and then to test something else, would be unethical. But rather than teaching to the test, the teacher is teaching to the outcomes and then assessing those outcomes.

The principal feature of summative assessment is that it counts, generally toward students' grades. However, although this is common practice, it presents some difficulties. If many students answer a particular test item incorrectly or incompletely, it points to a difficulty not with the *students* but with the *teaching*. That is, teachers must be prepared to accept the possibility that students' poor performance is not due to their own lack of industry, but to inadequacies in the teacher's own design of instruction or explanations of concepts.

Furthermore, many teachers have come to understand the power of the practice of marking "in pencil," that is, permitting students to revise their work following further instruction. Teachers of writing have long recognized the benefits of allowing students to revise their drafts and resubmit them; this is known as the *writing process* and typically involves many iterations before a final draft is turned in. This practice has many of the elements of formative assessment, discussed in the following section, and links with issues of grading, discussed in Chapter 11, "Grading Student Performance." But it serves to illustrate some of the challenges teachers face as they design summative assessments for classroom use. What is clear, however, is that teachers must find a way to balance the need for students to work hard to master important content with an environment of trust and fairness.

Types of Summative Assessments

But even given the challenges of designing effective summative assessments, much is known. As described in Chapter 2, "What We Know About Assessment," the forms of assessment used must be appropriate to the types of learning outcomes. Thus, for outcomes related to factual knowledge, a multiple-choice test is sufficient. The great benefit of true/false and multiple-choice tests is that the questions have (if the test is well designed) only one correct response. This feature makes them fast to score and yields a "clean" score, usually in the form of a number. In the measurement world, such test items are called *select* because the student picks, or selects, the correct answer. The advantages of this form of assessment are the wide range of knowledge that may be assessed (because students don't require much time to answer each question) and the speed of correcting such tests.

But other, and arguably more important, types of curriculum outcomes cannot be assessed through multiple-choice or true/false tests. For conceptual understanding, reasoning skills, languages, social skills, and the performing arts, more complex assessments are needed, those that engage students in creating an answer. In measurement terms, these are known as *constructed response* items. Thus, students might be asked to explain the relationship between buoyancy and density (or dictatorship and monarchy) in their own words; or to solve a mathematics problem and describe their strategy; or to write a persuasive essay convincing the school board to allocate funds for a school project. Such *performance tasks* are designed to elicit students' knowledge and skill; they require a more complex response than simply selecting the correct answer. Students are required to construct, or create, a response.

Performance Tasks and Rubrics

The essential first step in using performance assessment is to design the *task,* or what it is that students will be asked to do. Educators must decide what would serve to elicit student understanding; this might be an explanation of a scientific phenomenon in their own words, or a description of the factors that led to a historical event, or a solution to a mathematics problem showing the steps used in arriving at the answer. Such tasks need not require lengthy student responses, but they should get to the heart of what students have learned.

Educators must also decide whether the assessment, whatever it is, will be administered under *testing conditions,* that is, limited time, no access to materials, and so on. As explained in Chapter 2, "What We Know About Assessment," there are advantages to testing conditions, principally that the teacher can be sure that what the student submits is that student's own work. But there are circumstances where such anonymity is not possible, as when students complete a project in art class or play a passage on a musical instrument, both of which are, of necessity, public performances.

Developing a performance task that will enable students to reveal their level of understanding is only the first step in planning summative assessment; it is also essential to decide how students' work will be evaluated. For example, if students are asked to write a persuasive essay, how will the teacher know that a student's effort is adequate? It's not enough to read the essay and provide a global assessment such as B+. How is the B+ determined? How does the teacher decide? How will students, for that matter, know how their work will be evaluated so that they can direct their efforts accordingly? For these purposes, a scoring guide, or rubric, is needed.

The idea of a scoring guide is not complicated: Such a document identifies the important criteria by which student work will be evaluated and provides a brief description of performance at each of several levels of proficiency. The elements of a successful scoring guide or rubric are as follows:

> ***Clear criteria and standards.*** For an essay (either as part of a test or part of another assignment), a speech, or a lab report, teachers must establish, and make known to students, the criteria by which their work will be evaluated. For example, in an essay, the organization is probably important. But what about grammar? Use of expressive language? Paragraph structure?
>
> In fact, when students themselves help determine those criteria, they understand them better than when they are simply informed of them. Even young children (older than perhaps those in third grade) can be explicit about the characteristics of, for example, a good presentation to the class. They will identify such things as speaking sufficiently slowly and loudly, having a clear organization, using relevant examples, and the like. By knowing beforehand how their work will be evaluated, students are better able to address the criteria while completing the project, essay, or lab report or preparing for a presentation.

Public disclosure of the criteria and standards by which student work will be evaluated goes a long way toward eliminating the secrecy surrounding assessment that many educators experienced in their own school days. In fact, when the criteria and standards are explicit and agreed upon, the relationship between the teacher and students is transformed. This is dramatically the case when the assessment is an external one, such as an advanced-placement exam, but it can also be seen with classroom assessment. The teacher's role shifts from that of judge to that of partner. That is, rather than deciding, in secret, whether students have achieved proficiency in the curricular outcomes, as revealed through an assessment, the teacher and students work together to help the students' performance reach the agreed-upon standard. The teacher's role, then, is one of coach and advisor rather than judge and jury.

Levels of performance, or a rubric.   It's not sufficient to identify the criteria by which student work will be evaluated. It's also essential to be able to determine, for any piece of student work, whether the criteria have been met. The tool used for this effort is called a *scoring guide,* or *rubric,* and describes, in words, several levels of performance against which student work may be compared. This clarity about performance is essential for teachers, of course; it enables them to evaluate student work consistently against clear standards. But it helps students as well: Unless students understand clearly what excellence on the different criteria looks like (and this might well be different for students of different ages), they can't aim for it.

Two examples of rubrics for student essays are provided on the following pages. The first is technically a holistic rubric, although the elements for each point on the scale are des-cribed individually; the second is an analytic rubric. They may be adapted for students at different levels. An additional rubric for student group work follows.

There are a number of considerations when creating a rubric:

Is the rubric holistic or analytic?   A *holistic* rubric, as its name suggests, describes a student work product or performance in its totality. Thus, a level 2 essay, for example, would possess certain characteristics in terms of organization, use of language, and so on; these elements are combined into a single description. An *analytic* rubric, on the other hand, has descriptors for each element for each level of the rubric, presented separately. Figure 7.1 is an example of a holistic rubric, and Figure 7.2 is an example of an analytic rubric. Figure 7.3 is a second example of a holistic rubric.

The advantage of a holistic rubric is that it can be applied rather quickly to samples of student work; that is, a teacher can read, for example, a student essay and quickly determine whether it represents a level 2 or a level 4 performance. However, if a rubric is to be used to offer specific feedback to students, an analytic rubric is preferable because it provides more detailed information; students learn from the score precisely which aspects of their work need to be strengthened in order to qualify for the next level of performance on the rubric.

Weighting.   Are all the criteria equally important or are some more important than others? For example, is the organization of an essay or the use of correct syntax so essential that it trumps everything else? When using an analytic rubric, questions of weighting are not as important as they are with a holistic rubric, because it's possible to

At each of the six score points for on-topic papers, descriptors of writing performance are lettered as follows:

a = response to the topic
b = understanding and use of the passage
c = quality and clarity of thought
d = organization, development, and support
e = syntax and command of language
f = grammar, usage, and mechanics

Score of 6: Superior

A 6 essay shows superior writing but may have minor flaws.
   A typical essay in this category:

a. addresses the topic clearly and responds effectively to all aspects of the task
b. demonstrates a thorough critical understanding of the passage in developing an insightful response
c. explores the issues thoughtfully and in depth
d. is coherently organized and developed, with ideas supported by apt reasons and well-chosen examples
e. has an effective, fluent style marked by syntactic variety and a clear command of language
f. is generally free from errors in grammar, usage, and mechanics

Score of 5: Strong

A 5 essay demonstrates clear competence in writing. It may have some errors, but they are not serious enough to distract or confuse the reader.
   A typical essay in this category:

a. addresses the topic clearly but may respond to some aspects of the task more effectively than others
b. demonstrates a sound critical understanding of the passage in developing a well-reasoned response
c. shows some depth and complexity of thought
d. is well organized and developed, with ideas supported by appropriate reasons and examples
e. displays some syntactic variety and facility in the use of language
f. may have a few errors in grammar, usage, and mechanics

Score of 4: Adequate

A 4 essay demonstrates adequate writing. It may have some errors that distract the reader, but they do not significantly obscure the meaning.
   A typical essay in this category:

a. addresses the topic but may slight some aspects of the task
b. demonstrates a generally accurate understanding of the passage in developing a sensible response
c. may treat the topic simplistically or repetitively
d. is adequately organized and developed, generally supporting ideas with reasons and examples
e. demonstrates adequate use of syntax and language
f. may have some errors but generally demonstrates control of grammar, usage, and mechanics

FIGURE 7.1   CSU English Placement Test Scoring Guide

Score of 3: Marginal

A 3 essay demonstrates developing competence but is flawed in some significant way(s).
   A typical essay in this category reveals one or more of the following weaknesses:

a. distorts or neglects aspects of the task
b. demonstrates some understanding of the passage but may misconstrue parts of it or make limited use of it in developing a weak response
c. lacks focus, or demonstrates confused or simplistic thinking
d. is poorly organized and developed, presenting generalizations without adequate and appropriate support or presenting details without generalizations
e. has limited control of syntax and vocabulary
f. has an accumulation of errors in grammar, usage, and mechanics that sometimes interfere with meaning

Score of 2: Very Weak

A 2 essay is seriously flawed.
   A typical essay in this category reveals one or more of the following weaknesses:

a. indicates confusion about the topic or neglects important aspects of the task
b. demonstrates very poor understanding of the main points of the passage, does not use the passage appropriately in developing a response, or may not use the passage at all
c. lacks focus and coherence and often fails to communicate its ideas
d. has very weak organization and development, providing simplistic generalizations without support
e. has inadequate control of syntax and vocabulary
f. is marred by numerous errors in grammar, usage, and mechanics that frequently interfere with meaning

Score of 1: Incompetent

A 1 essay demonstrates fundamental deficiencies in writing skills.
   A typical essay in this category reveals one or more of the following weaknesses:

a. suggests an inability to comprehend the question or to respond meaningfully to the topic
b. demonstrates little or no ability to understand the passage or to use it in developing a response
c. is unfocused, illogical, or incoherent
d. is disorganized and undeveloped, providing little or no relevant support
e. lacks basic control of syntax and vocabulary
f. has serious and persistent errors in grammar, usage, and mechanics that severely interfere with meaning

FIGURE 7.1   CSU English Placement Test Scoring Guide *(continued)*

comment on each aspect of the student's performance separately from the others. Thus, an essay might be judged a level 2 for organization and a level 3 for its use of syntax.

How many points on the scale?   As a general rule, an even number of points is preferable to an odd number for the simple reason that many people, when applying a rubric, tend to "go to the middle," a practice called *central tendency* by measurement experts. An odd number of points on the scale prevents that practice. Most rubrics are written with four distinct levels of performance.

	Level One	**Level Three**	**Level Five**
Ideas	As yet, the paper has no clear sense of purpose or central theme. To extract meaning from the text, the reader must make inferences based on sketchy or missing details. The writing reflects more than one of these problems.	The writer is beginning to define the topic, even though development is still basic or general.	This paper is clear and focused. It holds the reader's attention. Relevant anecdotes and details enrich the central theme, though not required.
Organization	The writing lacks a clear sense of direction. Ideas, details, or events seem strung together in a loose or random fashion; there is no identifiable internal structure. The writing reflects more than one of these problems.	The organizational structure is strong enough to move the reader through the text without too much confusion.	The organization enhances and showcases the central idea or theme. The order, structure, or presentation of information is compelling and moves the reader through the text.
Voice	The writer seems indifferent to the topic and the content. The writing lacks purpose and audience engagement.	The writer seems sincere but not fully engaged or involved. The writing has a discernible purpose but is not compelling.	The writer speaks directly to the reader in a way that is individual, compelling, and engaging. The writer crafts the writing with an awareness and respect for the audience and the purpose for writing.
Word Choice	The writer demonstrates a limited vocabulary or has not searched for words to convey specific meaning.	The language is functional, even if it lacks much energy. It is easy to figure out the writer's meaning on a general level.	Words convey the intended message in a precise, interesting, and natural way. The words are powerful and engaging.
Sentence Fluency	The reader has to practice quite a bit in order to give this paper a fair interpretive reading.	The text hums along with a steady beat but tends to be more pleasant or businesslike than musical, more mechanical than fluid.	The writing has an easy flow, rhythm, and cadence. Sentences are well built, with strong and varied structure that invites expressive oral reading.

FIGURE 7.2   Six-Trait Writing Rubric—Northwest Regional Educational Laboratory

| **Conventions** | Errors in spelling, punctuation, capitalization, usage, and grammar and/or paragraphing repeatedly distract the reader and make the text difficult to read. | The writer shows reasonable control over a limited range of standard writing conventions. Conventions are sometimes handled well and enhance readability; at other times, errors are distracting and impair readability. | The writer demonstrates a good grasp of standard writing conventions (e.g., spelling, punctuation, capitalization, grammar, usage, paragraphing) and uses conventions effectively to enhance readability. Errors tend to be so few that just minor touch-ups would get this piece ready to publish. |
| **Presentation (Optional)** | The reader receives a garbled message due to problems relating to the presentation of the text. | The writer's message is understandable in this format. | The form and presentation of the text enhance the ability of the reader to understand and connect with the message. It is pleasing to the eye. |

FIGURE 7.2   Six-Trait Writing Rubric—Northwest Regional Educational Laboratory *(continued)*

There are variations, of course. Occasionally educators will create a rubric with, say, six points on the scale but write descriptors for only two of them, for example level 2 and level 5. Then, when evaluating a piece of student work, they determine whether it is more like the level 2 descriptor or the level 5 descriptor. If the statement precisely describes the work, then that is its level of performance, namely, level 2 or level 5. But if the work is below the level 2 statement, it is judged a level 1; above that performance, it is judged a level 3. The same practice is applied at the top levels of performance. If the work is below the level 5 statement, it is judged a level 4; above that performance, it is judged a level 6.

Distance between levels.   The distance between levels on a rubric (whether it is holistic or analytic) should be as equal as possible. That is, the distance between level 2 and level 3 should be similar to that between level 3 and level 4; the latter should not represent a large jump in performance.

Sample student work, or "anchor papers."   Students find it enormously helpful to see sample student work representing different levels of quality as a guide while doing their work. Thus, for students to see a level 2 essay and contrast it with others evaluated as level 3 and level 4 brings the rubric to life. And from the point of view of rubric development, it is usually essential to see samples of student work in order to be sure that the items in the rubric and the descriptors of the various levels actually reflect what students do.

Standard-setting or "cut score."   When preparing rubrics to evaluate student products and performances, it is essential to answer the question "How good is good enough?" That is, what level of performance would cause a teacher to take

---

4—Thorough Understanding

- Consistently and actively works toward group goals.
- Is sensitive to the feelings and learning needs of all group members.
- Willingly accepts and fulfills individual role within the group.
- Consistently and actively contributes knowledge, opinions, and skills.
- Values the knowledge, opinion, and skills of all group members and encourages their contribution.
- Helps the group identify necessary changes and encourages group action for change.

3—Good Understanding

- Works toward group goals without prompting.
- Accepts and fulfills individual role within the group.
- Contributes knowledge, opinions, and skills without prompting.
- Shows sensitivity to the feelings of others.
- Willingly participates in needed changes.

2—Satisfactory Understanding

- Works toward group goals with occasional prompting.
- Contributes to the group with occasional prompting.
- Shows sensitivity to the feelings of others.
- Participates in needed changes, with occasional prompting.

1—Needs Improvement

- Works toward group goals only when prompted.
- Contributes to the group only when prompted.
- Needs occasional reminders to be sensitive to the feelings of others.
- Participates in needed changes when prompted and encouraged.

FIGURE 7.3   Collaboration Rubric

remedial action? Many educators prepare four-level rubrics in which level 1 represents "not at all," level 2 represents "almost," level 3 represents "good enough," and level 4 represents "excellent." Of course, there are other ways of approaching this issue, but it's helpful to have an overall guide.

Evaluating Student Work

In evaluating student work using rubrics, collaboration among teachers is essential. Different individuals see student work differently, and everyone learns from the perspectives of others. And if rubrics are used for high-stakes summative assessments (as in an end-of-course exam), consistency in evaluating student work is absolutely essential. It would be unfair for student products or performances to be judged more leniently by one teacher than by another.

Furthermore, there is much to be learned by examining student work in addition to ascertaining the level of understanding of different students. For example, teachers can discover, in the patterns of student responses, that certain concepts were not adequately explained. Alternatively, from the responses of certain students, teachers can discover their levels of cognitive development, which may not be evident in classroom interactions.

FORMATIVE ASSESSMENT: USING ASSESSMENT IN INSTRUCTION

The use of assessment to guide learning is a relatively recent development in schools. Previously, a test signaled the *end* of instruction on a given unit of study. However, when used to guide instruction, assessment is an integral part *of* instruction. By enhancing their skill in the use of formative assessment, teachers add a powerful strategy to their repertoire.

The essential concept behind formative assessment is that students provide their teachers with multiple indications of their level of understanding through their day-to-day responses to assignments, through their answers to questions in class, and through the questions they themselves ask. By using these clues to adjust what they do next, teachers can respond to the needs of individuals and groups of students.

It should be noted that the criteria for student performance established and used in summative assessment to evaluate learning may also be used in formative assessment to guide learning. For example, writing rubrics, such as those described above, should be well known to students (perhaps even created with student input) and may be used on a daily basis to examine student essays and provide feedback. Indeed, students themselves can use the scoring guides or rubrics to plan their own efforts or to monitor their own learning. For example, when planning a group presentation, students can ensure that their own presentation satisfies the established criteria, for example, for organization, involving all group members in making the presentation, effective use of visuals, and so on.

Teacher-Directed Formative Assessment

The first beneficiaries, and the first people to make use of formative assessment information, are teachers. By being attuned to their students' experiences in learning, they can modify their approaches for groups of students or individuals. Rather than forging ahead when confronted with quizzical looks, teachers are able to make changes in what they are doing, in how they present new information, and in the instructional activities they devise for students.

In fact, the benefits of an approach called *mastery learning* have been evident for decades. First described by Benjamin Bloom (1984), mastery learning includes a phase in the instructional process in which teachers, acting on the results of a preliminary assessment, provide either corrective instruction or enrichment activities, thus ensuring that every student moves forward with adequate understanding of the curriculum. The results achieved by Bloom and his colleagues were truly dramatic; they did not achieve the same results in whole-class instruction that are attained in one-to-one tutoring, but they came very close. They demonstrated that it is possible, using focused formative assessment, to attain far higher levels of student achievement than had been thought possible. Not surprisingly, these ideas are back in vogue today, because they offer educators the promise of being able to break the cycle of low achievement and low self-esteem that plagues many schools.

The teacher's use of formative assessment also involves the type of feedback offered to students on their work. Of course, teachers use the results of informal observations of students and their work to adjust the way they teach those students. But in addition, they use their observations to provide suggestions to students on how their work could be improved. It's helpful if several guidelines are followed:

- Feedback should be timely. It's not helpful to tell students 3 weeks after they have submitted a paper how it could have been improved. Teachers must plan their schedules so that they can respond to student work, while it is still fresh in their minds, giving them guidance on how to proceed.
- Feedback to students must be specific and offer concrete ideas about how the work could be improved. Comparisons with other students' work should be avoided; this is a matter between the student and the teacher, with the teacher offering specific suggestions on where a student should focus his or her efforts.

Student-Directed Formative Assessment

It is when students take charge of the formative assessment process that its full power is displayed. In fact, the use of formative assessment by students has the potential to dramatically shift the nature of the student-teacher relationship. In a classroom where the only assessments are those given by the teacher, through what has been traditionally a secret process, many students respond by doing enough to get by, and others by competing, where they must, for the limited supply of gold stars, A's, or class ranking. In either case, the teacher holds the power and students know it; they therefore adopt a low-profile, low-risk strategy, looking for clues to the right answer and sometimes even refraining from asking a question in class if it might reveal that they lack understanding.

A critical aspect of student-directed formative assessment is student self-assessment. This is not optional or merely desirable; it is central to creating a classroom community in which students assume responsibility for their learning. Black et al. (2003) have noted that

> many pupils . . . appear to have become accustomed to receiving classroom teaching as an arbitrary sequence of exercises with no overarching rationale. To overcome this pattern of passive reception requires hard and sustained work. When pupils do acquire such an overview, they then become more committed and more effective as learners. Moreover, their own assessments become an object of discussion with their teachers and with one another, and this discussion further promotes the reflection on one's own thinking that is essential to good learning. (p. 6)

Jan Chappuis (2005) also comments on the central nature of student self-assessment and peer review as central to effective learning. She points out that one strategy to help students understand the criteria and levels of performance for their work, and to assess their own work, is to engage them first in evaluating anonymous student work. When students examine anonymous student essays, for example, against a scoring rubric and determine why one essay is strong whereas another is weak, they come to understand the criteria and the rubric well and can apply them in evaluating their own work. The anonymity is important, of course, because it ensures that student attention is focused on the work itself and not on the personalities of the individuals who produced it.

When students have acquired skill in assessing products, they can apply this skill to their own performance. For example, after writing a draft of an essay, students can evaluate it against the criteria in the rubric and even award themselves a score. More important than the score, however, are the insights students obtain from this exercise; it may become evident to them, for example, that their essay needs stronger descriptive language or better organization. Making those corrections on their own work can be a significant part of students' improvement in performance. In addition, students can learn to review one another's work and provide supportive feedback. This is a powerful strategy once students learn to do it well. For example, students can read one another's essays and comment on where ideas are not clear or where a classmate has not made a strong case for a position. Such self-regulation and assumption of responsibility for learning and performance is at the heart of a classroom organized as a community of learners.

Formative assessment by both teachers and students is at the heart of good teaching. It depends on developing carefully crafted questions and giving students sufficient time to produce thoughtful answers or well-planned products or performances. It also requires students' internalization of what constitutes high-quality work and a classroom culture that supports students taking responsibility to achieve that high quality. This does not happen by itself; it requires purposeful planning on the part of teachers. However, it is a strategy that pays large dividends, because it respects the autonomy and responsibility of students and builds on their own natural drive toward competence.

COMMENTARY ON THE INSTRUCTIONAL EXAMPLES

Both of the instructional examples illustrate how assessment can be used as a powerful ingredient in teaching.

How Many Beans?

In this elementary mathematics example, students provide the teacher with multiple opportunities to monitor their development of concepts and understanding. Different students approach the initial problem (how many beans are in a jar?) very differently: Some students tackle the problem impetuously, diving into a solution. Other students are more systematic and measured, weighing options carefully before suggesting a strategy.

In the course of discussing different approaches, students must engage in a multistep process of reasoning. For example, if they elect to use a "weight" approach to estimating the number of beans in the jar, they must decide which small measure (such as a portion cup) to use as a unit; they must count the number of beans in one unit and weigh those beans. Then they must weigh all the beans in the jar and determine how many units there are. Finally, they must calculate the number of beans in the jar by multiplying the number in one unit by the number of units. It is a challenge for some students to keep all this in mind while carrying out the process; a teacher can quickly determine, by circulating around the class, which students have developed the ability to engage in this type of systematic reasoning and which students still find it a challenge.

Furthermore, in circulating, and in hearing the reports of different groups of students, the teacher is able to ascertain which students are comfortable with applying computation skills to a practical situation. Some students seem to believe that the only purpose of multiplication, for example, is to complete a worksheet. But the skills of multiplication and of estimating the product of two numbers have many practical applications. (For example, when purchasing six ice cream cones, it is important to be able to estimate the approximate total cost so that the check, when it arrives, can be judged to be reasonable or not.)

A challenge in this unit, as in any unit in which students work in teams, is to determine from their work which students actually understand the concepts being taught and which ones are coasting along on the work of their classmates. This is not a matter of insisting that every student do the work. Instead, it's a matter of being sure that all students in a group actually understand what is being done. Some students, after all, are happy to let others take the lead and to hold back, or take direction from other members of their team, until the work is done. Unless the teacher is vigilant, the shaky nature of some students' understanding may not become evident until students have completed the summative assessment. However, by circulating and talking with students, teachers have the opportunity to evaluate their students' thinking and understanding and to encourage students to deepen their reasoning about the problem.

Of course, the summative assessment (for example, estimating the number of people in a crowd and explaining one's process for arriving at the answer) provides the teacher with evidence of each student's understanding. Since this estimate is done by each student individually, the teacher can determine the strengths of each student in this type of work and know which areas to emphasize in future tasks that involve estimation.

Pre-Revolutionary America

In the history example, students provide teachers with multiple indications of their level of understanding of the concepts involved, both as the unit is progressing and in their performance on the summative assessment.

First, as students generate questions for exploration, they reveal their insights into the period under study. As students suggest topics and questions to answer, teachers can ascertain the level of sophistication of their thinking and can, through the questions they ask as they circulate, help students deepen their approach. Some students may need assistance in narrowing their question for investigation; attempting to tackle too broad a topic is a difficulty that many students encounter in doing independent work.

While students are researching their questions and preparing their reports for presentation, teachers have multiple opportunities to ascertain the extent of their skills in investigation and to provide suggestions, as well as to ensure that all students are contributing to the overall effort of their group. In other words, there are no freeloaders in the joint effort.

The formal presentations by the different groups and the unit test provide, of course, the best summative information for the teacher on student mastery of the concepts and skills in the unit. But because the teacher's awareness of each student's progress has developed over the entire course of the unit, this is not a one-shot affair. However, it makes a highly significant contribution to the teacher's understanding of each student's level of performance.

Summary

Student assessment is at the heart of the specification of learning; it is through the assessments, after all, that the curriculum outcomes are operationalized. An outcome statement might state that students are able to solve two-step word problems. But that statement can have very different meanings in third grade, eighth grade, and Algebra II. Thus, the statement in the curriculum must be accompanied by an example of the specific type of problem—the size of the numbers, the cognitive rigor required by each of the steps, and so on. Providing those examples is fundamentally an assessment question.

The design of both summative and formative assessments is an important element of instructional planning. The assessment techniques used must be appropriate to the learning outcomes and should be accompanied by a scoring guide or rubric. Those tools may also be used as the foundation of informal assessment by both teachers and students.

Chapter 8

Designing Learning Experiences

The heart of education, as far as students are concerned, consists of the nature of the learning experiences they encounter. What is it that students are asked to *do* to master the complex content specified in the curriculum?

INTRODUCTION

While designing learning experiences for students, teachers make use of considerations discussed in earlier chapters in this book:

- What is it precisely that I want my students to learn? (Chapter 6, "Establishing Learning Outcomes")
- What do I know, in general, about how people learn and what my students are likely to find engaging? (Chapter 3, "What We Know About Student Learning")
- What do I know about motivation and how to enlist students' energies so that they will commit to the hard work required for significant learning? (Chapter 4, "What We Know About Motivation")
- What do I know about my particular students that will help me design effective learning experiences for them? (Chapter 5, "Knowing Our Students")

With these considerations in mind, teachers can design engaging activities that will result in the learning they desire among their students. Of course, experience plays an important role; once teachers have designed learning activities for a given series of instructional outcomes and a specific group of students, they will be able to use them, with some modification, in other classes or in other years. It is this fact, more than any other, that accounts for the stress of the first few years of teaching; new teachers must design every activity from scratch, with very little to fall back on.

In addition, if an instructional activity is not going well, those new to the profession tend not to have a "Plan B" that they can summon for service. Consequently, new teachers must frequently muddle through or soldier on even when they would like to make a midcourse correction.

Teachers have access to many resources as they design learning experiences: instructional materials and textbooks, state and district curriculum guides, and sample unit and lesson plans on the Internet. But all teachers must create or modify instructional plans, adapting ideas from elsewhere to the demands and requirements of their own students. Such flexibility, and the skill to both recognize and respond to changing classroom conditions, evolve with experience and the development of expertise.

DISTINCTION BETWEEN ACTIVITIES AND OUTCOMES

Some teachers, particularly those new to the profession, confuse activities with learning outcomes. That is, when asked what they are planning for a lesson, their answers will focus not on what the students will *learn* but on what they will *do*. That is, a teacher might respond that "the students are reading Chapter 5 and answering the questions at the end" or that the class is "doing *A Tale of Two Cities*." The question then is "What will the students learn as a result of reading Chapter 5 or studying *A Tale of Two Cities*?" Is the latter unit concerned with the historical setting of the novel, or with Dickens' use of imagery, plot structure, or characterization? As stated in Chapter 6, "Establishing Learning Outcomes," it's absolutely essential that teachers are clear about what they intend their students to learn. Learning outcomes refer to actual *learning,* what students will know and be able to do as a result of a learning experience or a series of learning experiences. The outcomes may be short- or long-term and may relate to factual or conceptual knowledge, thinking and reasoning, or attitudes. They may relate to a single discipline or several. However they are specified, clarity about the desired learning is essential; such clarity drives everything else about instructional design: the choice of activities, materials, methods of grouping students, homework assignments, and so on.

However, clarity about learning outcomes does not suggest that teachers should not give careful thought to the activities they design to support those outcomes. Indeed, the design of engaging learning experiences is at the heart of instructional design; it is through their activities, and their reflection on those activities, that students learn what teachers intend them to learn.

CONSIDERATIONS IN THE DESIGN OF LEARNING EXPERIENCES

Earlier chapters in this book provide the mental models for what teachers must consider when they design learning experiences and, taken together, provide the specifications for those learning experiences.

Learning Outcomes

As described above, the desired learning outcomes provide the essential context for the design of learning experiences; whatever we ask students to do must be purposeful. It must advance student understanding in the curriculum outcomes we have set. School does not (or should not) consist of a random set of activities unconnected to any larger purpose. Time in school is in short supply, so it's essential to use that time in the most productive manner.

Naturally, learning activities should appeal to students; they should be fun in that sense. But they should not be merely fun. If fun were sufficient, teachers could organize entire days as a series of games. At the very least, the learning experiences in which we ask students to be engaged should be directed to desired learning of the curriculum outcomes.

Even rather mundane-sounding learning outcomes can be used to design rich instructional activities. For example, if a lesson's purpose is for students to understand the different meanings of a collection of vocabulary words, the teacher may be tempted to ask students to look the words up in a dictionary and to write sentences using the words in their different senses. Alternatively, students could be asked to create little skits illustrating the different meanings of the words. The latter activity would not only call forth students' understanding of the words, but would also enlist their powers of invention and require them to engage in joint work with classmates. On the other hand, creating skits requires more time than does writing sentences, so the teacher must decide whether the extra time is justified by the (supposedly) more engaging activity of creating and performing skits.

Regardless, though, of the creativity of learning experiences, their one critical attribute is that they help students develop an understanding of the learning outcomes in the curriculum.

The Nature of Learning

Research on cognition has demonstrated conclusively the constructivist nature of learning: Students learn as a consequence of what they *do*. It is essential, therefore, that learning experiences engage students in *doing* things. That could include listening to a teacher's presentation, or watching a video, or other activities considered passive in nature. However, it's important to be aware of the *students'* experience in listening to an explanation or watching a video. If it is presented in such a manner that students can make connections or develop new insights, then they are intellectually active in the sense required by cognitive research.

As explained in Chapter 3, "What We Know About Student Learning," human beings, by their very nature, are intensely active intellectually. This intellectual activity begins in early childhood and may be observed even in babies; they are constantly putting ideas together, relating one observation to another, and making predictions as to what will happen next. They don't acquire this curiosity from the adults around them. It is completely innate; it is part of being human. Young children are models of eagerness when it comes to learning, the first few years of life resulting in an explosive expansion of cognitive capacity and conceptual understanding. They learn to talk, an impressive intellectual achievement requiring pattern recognition, separation and control of variables, and systematic experimentation. They don't learn these things from adults, but rather from trial and error. But learn they do, entering school with an impressive vocabulary and a well-developed sense of how the world works.

Given the intense natural intellectual activity of children and their drive to learn, the challenge for teachers is to direct that natural energy to the learning that is needed for school success. On their own, children might not choose to learn geography, for example, or other important aspects of state content standards. Teachers must capture students' natural desire to learn and turn it to their own purposes. In general, this means that teachers must find ways for students to be intellectually active, with the result of that activity being the desired learning.

Of course, children (particularly young children) are highly active physically as well; given a choice between a sedentary activity and a physical one, virtually all children will select the latter. Furthermore, many concepts that we want students to acquire in school, such as the concept of place value in elementary mathematics or the concept of buoyancy in science, are best taught through the use of manipulative materials for their modeling. However, the converse is not necessarily true. Students can use physical materials mindlessly and learn nothing from them. Thus, "hands-on" is not sufficient; learning in school must be "minds-on" as well. In other words, school is not a spectator sport for students; they must be busy understanding concepts, making connections, and creating new ways of looking at things. Teachers ensure this activity in their design of engaging learning experiences.

The Nature of Motivation

Human motivation has been widely studied, with a broad consensus having been reached on why people, children as well as adults, will invest energy in certain activities. These findings, together with their implications for the design of learning experiences, are summarized here.

In general, intrinsic motivation is more powerful than extrinsic motivation. When people engage in an activity because they want to do so, they are more motivated than if they are forced, or bribed by gold stars or grades, to do so. Furthermore, and paradoxically, when people are rewarded for an activity that they previously chose to do, they lose interest in it.

Intrinsic motivation is extremely powerful; it explains most of why people do what they do. When teachers can tap into students' natural drive for learning, their classes take on an energy that is simply not available otherwise. Thus, the contributors to intrinsic motivation and their implications for the design of instructional activities are reviewed here.

- Students need to feel connections to other people, particularly other students. They need to feel valued, and they need to have friends. This suggests that group work is more motivating to students than individual work. In their groups, students need to feel that they are making a contribution, one that is valued by others.

  Group work presents challenges for teachers, of course. It's important to create groups in which all students can participate and no students can coast on the strength of others. And given the inevitable range of students in every class, this requires thoughtful planning.

  However, the essential message is clear: Given a choice between an activity that students complete on their own and one they complete (or at least work on) in groups, group work is preferable. Even when teachers ask students to work independently, many students will find ways to interact with their classmates, talking quietly, passing notes, sending text messages, and so on. This drive to be with others is powerful, and teachers may as well build it into their instructional design.

- Students (in fact, all people) are strongly motivated to be competent. This drive helps explain why children will spend many hours perfecting their skill on the skateboard or playing a videogame or why people (primarily adults) become addicted to crossword puzzles or Sudoku. There is no extrinsic reward for the mastery of such skills and activities, only the satisfaction of having done them.

  This finding has implications for the design of instructional experiences and the resulting interaction between teachers and students. It is far more satisfying to solve a challenging problem, for example, than a trivial one or to recognize an aspect of a work of literature that goes beyond literal reading of the text. Challenging students to do such things and recognizing the significance of what they have accomplished is highly motivational for further efforts.

  Of course, learning experiences that pose too great a challenge for students can prove discouraging. The answer to this dilemma is to create learning experiences that present several levels of challenge simultaneously and to encourage students to take on as difficult a challenge as possible so that they can enjoy the satisfaction, the power, of mastering it. For example, a teacher could pose a mathematics problem and encourage students (either individually or in groups) to tackle it. If one student finds the answer quickly while others are still working on it, the teacher can pose a series of more challenging questions:

  > Are there any other answers or is this the only one? How do you know that?
  > Is there more than one method that can be used in solving this problem? What are all the possible ways?
  > Is there one best way to arrive at the answer? Is one approach more efficient or more sure-footed than others?

- Part of being human is the need for autonomy, for freedom. No one likes being told what to do; the drive for self-reliance helps explain the historical evolution of democratic structures of government. In the classroom, students prefer to choose what they do rather than learn in an authoritarian environment. Thus, learning experiences in which students can select from a menu of options are likely to be far more motivating than those presented with no choice.

Of course, when students are offered a choice among learning experiences, it's essential that any choice made be acceptable to the teacher. The opportunity is a hollow one if students discover that, having made a choice, they are not permitted to pursue it. Thus, when designing learning experiences, teachers should make sure that all of the choices offered yield the desired learning. In this way, teachers can get the greatest commitment from students in their work. Thus, after studying, for example, *The Old Man and the Sea*, students might be asked to write a brief essay in the style of Hemingway. The topic may be of the students' own choosing, but the style should reflect that of the novel they have been studying.

The Particular Students

Every class is different from every other. All classes consist of individuals, each with his or her own interests, talents, cultural heritage, and intriguing ideas. In addition, classes have personalities; particularly as they advance through the grades, groups of students acquire a reputation for being inventive, or for working hard, or for being competitive, or for getting into trouble. Of course, as with individuals, class reputations can persist even when the classes themselves change. For example, a class might have acquired a reputation for stretching the truth whenever possible. Afterward, students in that class might find that adults in the school tend not to believe their version of an account of an event, even when they are being completely honest.

But regardless of the reputation of an entire class, it is the individual students in their own class whom teachers must consider when designing learning experiences. Taking the time to learn about one's students' interests and strengths can pay large dividends in terms of student commitment and energy for learning. For example, some students are keenly interested in music or sports. These interests can either be incorporated directly into class assignments or used to illustrate certain points of a lesson.

The educational literature is filled with illustrations of this point; most teachers can tell stories of students who suddenly became committed to their schoolwork when it was designed to accommodate a particular interest. For example, an English teacher was finding it difficult to convince a student to develop a disciplined approach to nonfiction writing. However, when she discovered the student's passion for and knowledge of the theatre, she was willing to devote much energy to educating her, through her writing, on the fine points of acting.

Individual students have very different degrees of readiness for school experiences. Cognitive psychology has clearly demonstrated that children's' mental structures develop according to a consistent pattern over time and that prior to the acquisition of a certain structure, intellectual concepts that depend on that structure cannot be understood. And given that any class contains students who represent a wide range of cognitive developmental levels, teachers must accommodate to that range by offering learning experiences that make varying demands on cognitive sophistication. Alternatively, teachers must group students for collaborative work in such a way that they are able to serve as resources for one another.

Furthermore, individual students come to school from a range of family circumstances, some of them very challenging. For this reason, teachers must know, as part of their professional responsibilities, what community services are available to help students who may need them. Such services may be either physical or emotional; some students lack warm clothes for the winter or may live in chaotic home situations. Although they cannot address such conditions directly, teachers' awareness of them encourages them to be flexible in the demands they make of students and the support they offer. Some students have important responsibilities at home, such as caring for younger siblings or preparing the evening meal, or they may not have a quiet place in which to complete homework. Teachers may need to offer support after school to enable such students to keep up with the class and to take full advantage of their natural potential for learning.

Students' diverse cultural heritages provide opportunities for teachers to connect with their students. At the very least, they must demonstrate respect for students' cultural traditions; in other situations, they may find that they can incorporate students' backgrounds into what is being learned by the class as a whole.

When teachers make the effort to learn everything they can about their students, they demonstrate respect and caring for them. Most adults can recall teachers who made a significant impact on their own emerging sense of self. When teachers are positive, they can turn around a life. When they are negative, they do incalculable damage. Teachers are the most important adults, after parents and other close family members, in the lives of most students. It's important that teachers make the most of these relationships, using them to connect with students as individuals and to design learning experiences that will engage them in meaningful learning.

CHARACTERISTICS OF ENGAGING LEARNING EXPERIENCES

The implications for teachers of the research, and of commonsense knowledge, of how students learn and how they are motivated, are profound. Of course, all learning experiences should yield important student learning in the curriculum. But given what we know about learning and motivation, we can establish certain *specifications* for such learning experiences. In short, any activity in which students are engaged should be inherently interesting, provide choice and an opportunity to work collaboratively, and result in important learning. This is a tall order for teachers, but the result is students who are intrinsically motivated, reflecting the natural curiosity and energy for learning that are characteristic of even very young children.

This research suggests that teachers should attempt to create learning experiences for students that

- Provide students with interesting "puzzles" needing solutions. Such activities recognize that curiosity is a powerful motivator; to the extent that learning tasks invite students to solve a problem, explain incongruous events, or understand anomalies, students are driven by an innate curiosity to pursue such challenges.
- Provide students with opportunities to think and reason things through, to be creative, to analyze information, and to recognize patterns and connections. In other words, students have opportunities to think, and they are expected to do so.
- Offer students an opportunity to work together, because being with their friends is an important reason why many students come to school.
- Allow students some choice in what they will do. Choice offers students a sense of control over their lives and freedom from what may seem to be a teacher's unreasonable and arbitrary use of power.

In addition:

- When interacting with students, teachers must be sure that their students understand that they care deeply about them and their future. Some of this caring can take the form of knowing something about their lives beyond the classroom: their families or their nonacademic interests. In other situations, it suggests simultaneously setting high standards for academic work and expressing confidence that the students will be able to achieve those standards.
- When offering feedback to students, teachers should refrain from praising them for their intelligence or talent. Instead, they should offer praise for their hard work, persistence, and use of innovative strategies. In addition, by enabling students to see that what they have been learning and doing represents an important achievement, they allow students to experience the feelings of power and competence that accompany successful accomplishment of challenging work.

HOMEWORK

One application of the principles of engaging learning experiences for students is the matter of homework. Should teachers assign homework or not? This question is deceptively simple and has no simple answer. In fact, the subject of homework can provoke heated debate among educators, and between educators and the public, primarily parents. However, it's important for teachers to think it through carefully and to have a well-reasoned philosophy on the matter. This section outlines the factors teachers should consider when framing their own approach to homework.

Purpose(s) of Homework

Whether homework is considered to be a good thing or not frequently is determined by what one considers its purpose to be. The fact that homework is a ritual in most schools is not a sufficient reason to assign it. So, what is its purpose, and is that purpose justified?

EXTENDING THE SCHOOL DAY   Compared with students in many other nations, American students spend relatively little time in school. And when one considers that of the time allocated to class time, the actual academic learning time is only one third to one half, the time available for learning is even less than the allocated time. Therefore, one purpose of homework is to provide additional time for students to learn.

Of course, homework assignments must be suitable for independent work at home. Not everything qualifies, but teachers can make a strong case for homework assignments that involve activities such as writing, reading, memorizing vocabulary words, practicing a procedure in mathematics, or writing a science lab report. If students have the skills to do these activities, there is no reason why they must be done during class time. Homework assignments, of course, require high-quality learning, an issue dealt with below.

CONSOLIDATION OF LEARNING   Well-designed homework assignments can help students solidify their understanding and achieve mastery of important content. For example, once students have learned the different types of polynomials and strategies for factoring them, a homework assignment requiring them to recognize examples of the different types in order to factor them can consolidate their understanding of the patterns at work. This is a matter for practice; students must have attained conceptual understanding, but once they have done so, practice is what is needed.

ENCOURAGING STUDENT SELF-DISCIPLINE   Many teachers hold that a reasonable amount of homework requires that students develop self-discipline and skills of time management. Students, after all, have limited time after school, and if they are involved in out-of-school activities or if they hold a job, that time is even more limited. Therefore, in order to complete homework assignments, students must use their time wisely, and they must exercise the self-discipline to get it done rather than squander their time on frivolous activities.

Of course, some students don't have the time to complete homework assignments. If they hold a job after school, and particularly if the income from the job makes an important contribution to the family's finances, they may simply not have the hours available. This situation seriously undermines the ability of schools to engage students in sustained learning of complex content.

Age of the Students

It is generally accepted that homework is unsuitable for young children. In fact, many people bemoan what they regard as the loss of childhood; some students' lives are highly programmed, leaving them little unstructured time. But even elementary students can benefit from some assignments to be completed at home, particularly if the assignments take advantage of the home environment—for example, interviewing neighbors about a proposed change in local zoning.

Suitability and Quality of the Assignments

Many education critics argue that homework should be abolished because it imposes needless stress on students and consists of stupid "busywork" assignments. However, what such critics are attacking is not homework per se but bad homework. That is, some assignments are, in fact, not worth doing and appear to have been assigned only to ask students to do something at home.

On the other hand, as a way to extend learning time and to permit students to complete work for which the school day is insufficient, homework can play an important role. But the assignments must be suitable both to the age of the students and for independent completion. Appropriate assignments include such things as writing a first draft of an essay, practicing lines for a play, or conducting Internet research in an investigation.

Parental Assistance

It's essential that students be able to complete homework assignments on their own. When parents are obliged to lend a hand with homework, they become, in effect, tutors, a role that not all parents are comfortable playing.

Not all parents are able to assist their children with homework. They may not have the skill to do so. Alternatively, their own lives may be so stressful that they simply don't have the time to sit down with their children to complete an assignment. Furthermore, if children have difficulty with an assignment and a parent tries to help, frustration can ensue if the efforts are unsuccessful. Such frustration does not contribute to a healthy relationship between parents and children.

An additional problem with parental assistance is that for large assignments, the parent's contribution may constitute a significant portion of the final product, so teachers have no way of assessing what students have learned from, for example, a science project. This is a problem of authenticity; assignments that count as a significant portion of students' grades must be completed by the students themselves.

The Opportunity Cost of Homework

Some parents point out that if their children did not have such a heavy load of homework, they could make much more valuable use of their time after school and on weekends. Indeed, some students have the opportunity, with their families, to engage in very interesting and valuable activities, such as travel, working on a farm, or visiting museums. Thus, there is a genuine opportunity cost associated with homework in the form of other activities that can't be pursued due to lack of time.

In most families, however, this is not a serious consideration, and scheduling time for homework is an important aspect of time management for students to master. But where it is an issue, it is important for teachers, in consultation with students and their parents, to work out a suitable approach. Few would argue that a student should not be permitted to go on an exciting excursion because an assignment is due. However, a teacher may need to adjust the assignment's due date to accommodate the opportunity.

Encouraging Students to Complete Homework

In order for students to make a commitment to completing homework, two conditions must prevail: discipline and a perception of value. First, students must have the discipline to complete their homework; this means scheduling adequate time and resisting the temptation to pursue other possible activities. Completing homework must be seen as nonnegotiable (except in extraordinary circumstances), requiring the student to set aside time for it, free of other distractions.

But just as important, students must appreciate homework for its contribution to their learning and understanding. That is, homework must be seen as valuable. Students are quick to notice when an assignment seems foolish or when they believe that they are going through the motions for a skill that they have mastered. Homework must have perceived value; otherwise, why (other than avoiding the wrath of the teacher) should students do it?

Teachers can contribute to both aspects of students' willingness to complete homework. Some students may need help in getting organized to do it, particularly those students with challenging home environments. Coaching by a teacher can provide real help. But even students with supportive home environments may need some coaching and techniques suggested by other students in how to get organized, what to do when they encounter difficulties, and so on.

As for the perceived value of homework, teachers control the quality of assignments. And when students are asked for their opinions about the value of an assignment, they develop more ownership of the process than they would have otherwise. The teacher is, of course, the adult in the situation, the one assigning the homework. But when students realize that their teachers value their opinion on the worth of assignments, they develop an increasing commitment to the relationship and the learning that ensues.

COMMENTARY ON THE INSTRUCTIONAL EXAMPLES

The instructional examples offer illustrations of many of the principles described in this chapter.

How Many Beans?

Many of the activities in this unit are designed to maximize students' energy and commitment to learning. As a start, the initial question is intriguing: When students are asked to guess how many beans are in a jar, their answers tend to vary widely. So, the notion that it is possible to make a reasonably accurate estimate without counting is intriguing. And the idea that there are a variety of ways to arrive at an answer, and that the different approaches can be compared, is interesting.

In this unit of study, students cooperate with classmates to work through an approach to the problem. This group work, like all group work, is appealing to students; it enables them to interact with their friends while completing a class assignment. From the point of view of their learning, group work also reinforces a number of important concepts. First, students discover that several heads are better than one; their classmates may suggest an idea that they had never thought of. Second, in working together, students must develop the skills of collaboration, of listening, and of dividing the work in an efficient manner.

In working through a method for estimating the number of beans in the jar, students must engage in sustained, thoughtful work. The different methods (using volume, area, weight, etc.) all require several steps for their successful completion. They are also well served by a systematic approach; without such an approach, students can easily lose their way and forget where they are in the process. Thus, by engaging in the unit, students both develop and practice their thinking and reasoning skills within the context of an enjoyable, challenging, and interesting, problem to be solved.

Of course, students have a great deal of choice in this unit. They select among several approaches to use in solving the problem. They determine how to proceed using the method they have selected. Ultimately, of course, they learn that some approaches are more accurate or efficient than others. But the comparisons are between the *methods,* not between the *students.* Thus, these insights can inform students' choices in the future, helping them develop a powerful and flexible understanding of the mathematics of estimation.

Pre-Revolutionary America

The unit begins with students generating questions regarding the signers of the Declaration of Independence; this activity taps into their natural curiosity about human affairs. Why would a number of individuals in the British colonies risk their lives to declare their independence from the mother country? What effect did this act of defiance have on the relationships among these individuals and other important persons, such as members of their families? What were they risking in economic as well as personal terms?

The questions investigated as part of this unit hold intrinsic interest for students; they are particularly appropriate for high school students, who are keenly interested in issues of ethics and of the possible effect of small shifts in the course of events. Adolescents are intellectually equipped to investigate "what if?" questions or the question "Who was right in this situation?" or "How did the actions of the rebels look to the British loyalists?" These explorations are powerful. They help reinforce the idea that there is nothing inevitable about the course of events and that, even today, how events unfold is a consequence of how individuals behave and what actions they take.

In pursuing their own investigations and in hearing about the work of their classmates, students acquire a number of facts about the period before and during the Revolutionary War. They are then able to see the events of that age as part of a larger tapestry, yet shaped by the particular details of the period.

In working with classmates students acquire a better understanding of history, because all individuals bring their own strengths and perspectives. No one in the group has a monopoly on the good ideas; everyone's understanding is deepened when informed by multiple perspectives. Furthermore, students learn the skills of collaboration, of sharing responsibility, of careful listening, and of dividing the work. These are skills that will serve them well throughout their lives.

The design of this unit incorporates the principle of choice in instructional planning; students, after all, choose the question they will investigate. The challenge for the teacher, of course, is to ensure that regardless of the questions chosen by different groups of students, the consequence, for those students and for the class as a whole, will be an increased understanding of the pre–Revolutionary War period. To that end, teachers may have to help students adjust their initial questions so that they will allow rich investigations and discussion.

The very nature of this unit also encourages students to develop and apply their skills in thinking and reasoning. Depending on the question they select, they will analyze information, discern patterns in events, or formulate hypotheses regarding cause and effect. And even if each group's question does not require all of these thinking skills, every student will observe the effects of their use in the work of other groups.

All in all, the unit on the pre–Revolutionary War period enables high school students to "do history," to formulate and answer important questions about a period of time with enormous implications for the further development of the United States. It provides students an important window on the work of historians and the methods by which they work. Furthermore, they acquire important insights into a critical period of U.S. history, one with consequences that persist to this day.

Part 3

USING WHAT WE KNOW TO CREATE AN ENVIRONMENT FOR LEARNING

Designing engaging learning experiences is critical in promoting student learning. But it is not sufficient; establishing an environment in which that learning can occur is also necessary. Students cannot learn well if they are not simultaneously supported and challenged or if their classroom is in chaos.

There are many skills involved in creating a positive classroom environment for learning, and at first glance, they may appear to be in conflict—or at least in tension—with one another. On the one hand, students must feel honored and supported, suggesting a soft tone. On the other hand, classrooms are purposeful places, with no time to waste on frivolous activities. Teachers must walk the line between heavy and light, between hard and soft. They do this through the procedures they establish with students for classroom routines and student conduct. They also do it in the manner of their interactions with students, finding a compromise between sternness—insisting on high-quality work, for example—and building understanding with students so that they are able to do their best work.

All of the considerations discussed in Part 1 come into play as teachers create a learning environment. They must bear in mind the need for students to be actively involved in classroom decisions affecting their daily life in school. They must never forget the natural desire of students—indeed, of all people—to learn and achieve mastery of complex content. They must also consider the need for acceptance by others and for the security of predictable routines. All of these factors come into play as teachers establish their classrooms as productive environments conducive to learning and supportive of students.

Chapter 9

A Safe, Respectful, and Challenging Learning Environment

When adults recall their school experiences after many years, what they tend to remember most vividly are the interactions with their teachers and with other students. This is remarkable: Teachers, when beginning their practice, focus, as they should, on instructional matters, that is, on how to design engaging learning experiences for their students. But the students themselves, even many years later, recall a teacher's encouragement or disparagement. They remember ridicule from classmates or a teacher's prompting them to put forth their best effort. Long after the details of chemistry have faded, most people will remember, sometimes in astonishing detail, events that happened in a classroom years (sometimes 30 or 40, depending on their age) ago.

Given the power of classroom interactions in shaping the nature of students' school experience, it is important for teachers to unpack the different components of those interactions and to ensure that they structure them in such a manner as to yield the greatest benefit for their students.

A SAFE AND RESPECTFUL ENVIRONMENT

Above all, a school environment (including classrooms, corridors, lunchrooms, and playgrounds) must be safe for students. This requirement includes both physical and psychological safety and extends to students' treatment by teachers and other students. Student safety in corridors, lunchrooms, and playgrounds is a matter for the entire faculty of a school to ensure; classroom safety, however, is the responsibility of the individual teacher.

Physical Safety

Physical safety is a primary feature of every classroom; teachers must ensure that students' well-being is not put at risk by the arrangement of furniture, dangling electrical cords, or disorganized traffic patterns. Chemicals must be stored in a responsible manner and students instructed in their use. Parents must feel sure that when their children go off to school, they will be safe from physical harm.

Some teachers adopt a highly cautious attitude toward the physical safety of their students with the intention of avoiding all possible risks. To that end, they prohibit the use of scissors or other sharp instruments or the use of materials that might, under any circumstances, cause physical harm. They observe correctly that students are curious creatures, likely to explore anything they encounter. Children, depending on their age, want to know whether physical objects float or sink, what sound they make when hit together, or whether a stack of them will tumble down. When children experiment in this way, they are not being (or not intending to be) destructive; they are merely curious. Thus, depriving students of opportunities to experiment with physical materials runs counter to their natural ways of being.

Science class, of course, presents the most potentially dangerous environment. Students work with chemicals that could corrode the skin or cause blindness; they may handle a flaming Bunsen burner or use sharp knives. These hazards are real, and teachers are well advised to be aware of them. But more mundane physical dangers are always present: students racing around the classroom, or opening a door suddenly to hit another student's face, or tripping on something left on the floor. A completely risk-free environment is a sterile environment and cannot be achieved in an actual classroom.

Therefore, rather than attempt to establish an environment that poses no possible physical risk to students, teachers can create a safe environment by teaching students how to make it so. Learning to handle dangerous tools safely is an important aspect of competence and maturity; every child knows that being allowed to carry scissors, use sharp instruments, or handle chemicals represents an adult's trust in his or her ability to do it safely. But, as with other aspects of learning, children aren't born knowing how to do such things properly; they must be taught. Similarly, students can be made aware of the dangers to themselves and others inherent in moving quickly around the classroom or leaving items on the floor.

Hence, lessons on physical safety may be conducted in the same manner as any other lessons, and they vary, of course, depending on the age and maturity of the students. Thus, young children can act out what could happen if they fall while holding scissors pointing upward, using a soft material such as a pipe cleaner. Teachers of older students might help them build on what they know about fire or splashing liquids to derive safety guidelines for the use of Bunsen burners or chemicals. The results of these discussions with students of all ages are commonsense rules governing student conduct. These rules could, but probably need not, be formulated in writing and posted on the wall. But, critically, if students are observed violating these guidelines, they would temporarily lose the privilege of working with the material independently.

Psychological Safety

Beyond physical safety, it's essential that students feel emotionally safe in school. They must have an environment in which they are free to take risks—to suggest an idea without fear of ridicule or sarcasm from either the teacher or other students. The psychologically safe environment, then, is a matter of interactions, both between teacher and students and among students. Those interactions must be characterized by respect and an atmosphere of rapport.

When, years later, adults recall their school experiences, what frequently stands out in their minds is the way they were treated. They will often remember a teacher's support of them or a teacher's efforts to help them when they were struggling to understand something. Or, conversely, they may recall a teacher's sarcastic comment or a student's put-down more vividly than the concepts being learned. Thus, it is an essential part of the responsibility of every teacher to ensure that students experience a psychologically safe environment in which they are respected and trusted by everyone else in the class.

Teachers, particularly when they are beginning their practice, may need to make a strong effort to treat their students with respect. It's not that new teachers don't respect their students, but they may not be aware of how even an apparently "throwaway" comment might be interpreted by students. They may not be aware, in other words, of the power they wield and how seriously some students may interpret even a casual remark. Even experienced teachers can benefit from feedback from colleagues as they work to strengthen their support of students. Contemporary American society, as reflected in television sit-coms, is characterized by the casual put-down, with the most sarcastic comments receiving the biggest laughs. When both students and teachers internalize such interactions, it can be difficult to recognize the hurt that may be caused.

In addition to monitoring their own interactions with students, teachers have an obligation to teach their students to show respectful support of one another. These are skills that may be taught as readily as other skills, whether curriculum based (such as the skills of problem solving) or dealing with management issues (such as the skills of moving from one activity to another without causing collisions). Students can (and should) learn how to listen respectfully to their classmates and how to disagree politely with them. By reflecting on how they themselves feel when others treat a comment of theirs with disdain (through rolling of the eyes or other shows of disrespect), they can learn to monitor their own behavior. And once such lessons have been conducted, everyone in the class—students as well as the teacher—can be alert to such behavior and can point it out when they see it.

A CHALLENGING ENVIRONMENT

But although schools and classrooms must be safe, although the atmosphere must be warm and comfortable, that is not sufficient for learning to take place. A student's experience in school is not, after all, the intellectual equivalent of taking a hot bath. Within the atmosphere of safety and trust, students must be challenged to think, to make connections, and to derive general principles.

Part of the challenge of an environment derives from the nature of the tasks them-selves; they should be designed to engage students in high-level learning and thinking. But beyond that, teachers must be able to create and sustain an environment in which high-level performance is both expected and supported. The interactions, in other words, between teachers and students must be challenging within an overall atmosphere of emotional and intellectual support.

Teachers convey the environment of challenge through many specific actions in addition to the nature of the tasks and activities they assign to students. These are described briefly below.

Carefully Watching and Listening to Students

Alert teachers are aware of what their students know and how they are thinking. They know these things through formal means such as their students' performance on classroom and external tests and other assessments. But in addition, teachers must watch and listen carefully to what their students say and do. A quizzical look conveys confusion, as does a question that might seem to come from "left field."

Providing an appropriately challenging environment for each student requires knowing where students are in their learning and then structuring one's interactions accordingly. This requires continual diagnosis of students' progress and ascertaining what would constitute a suitable challenge, stretching students' thinking and understanding. It's possible to miss the mark in both directions: Teachers' questions and interactions sometimes assume too little learning on the part of students and sometimes too much. Only by watching and listening carefully can teachers know what would constitute an appropriate challenge.

Posing Appropriate Questions to Students

An important skill of good teaching is to pose high-level questions to students. This involves asking questions at an *appropriate* level of challenge. That level is different for different students and on different occasions. And in the course of a single lesson, the cognitive level of questions typically evolves. For example, in a literature class the teacher might begin a sequence of questions by asking "What happened next?" (a literal question).

The ensuing discussion might then be followed by the question "Why do you think _____ responded the way she or he did? Why do you think so? What evidence can you cite from the text for that view?" (an interpretive question). This could be followed by "What do you think might have happened if _____? What makes you predict that?" (a hypothetical question). These questions relate only to the plot and characterization. A similar series of questions could be constructed around the setting, the plot structure, or the symbolism embodied in any of the elements of the work.

With a group of students and with an individual student over a period of time, a teacher will pose a series of questions inviting ever-higher thinking and analysis. A teacher's skill is reflected in the ability to formulate these questions at different levels of challenge and know when to use each level. In a cognitively challenging environment, students will feel simultaneously stretched and supported. Stretching is built into the questions posed by the teacher; these are formulated in such a manner as to cause students to develop hypotheses and to make new connections among previously known facts and concepts. Thus, a teacher might begin a discussion of the American Revolution with a series of factual questions, such as the sequence of events preceding the signing of the Declaration of Independence, to establish that the students understood what happened. This might be followed by questions about the Tories in the colonies and how their loyalties were divided (interpretation), followed by questions as to what might have happened if, for example, the Battle of Princeton had gone the other way (hypothesis).

Responding to Student Questions and Answers

But it's not only the questions teachers ask that create a challenging environment; a teacher's responses to students also contribute to it. If the environment is safe, students will feel free to ask and respond to questions without fear of ridicule from either the teacher or other students. But a teacher's unconditional acceptance of any student contribution can inhibit deeper thinking. If a teacher responds to a student's superficial response to a question with "That's right!" or "What a good suggestion!" then other students learn that virtually any answer will do and that they can excel by simply participating in class discussions.

Instead, through their responses to students' questions and comments, teachers establish the level of cognitive challenge in the class. Thus, a teacher might respond, "Oh, yes, that's an interesting thought. Can you think of why that might be the case?" and if the original student cannot think of a response, the teacher can invite an idea from another student. Or, in the discussion of a science question, the teacher might inquire, "Is that the only possibility? Are you sure?" or "Is there another way we might think about this? Which approach would explain the greatest number of situations?"

A specific illustration of teachers' response to students is in their use of praise. As was pointed out in Chapter 4, "What We Know About Motivation," the use of praise can, paradoxically, undermine students' effort and their commitment to high-quality work. This is counterintuitive; one would think that praising a student's work would encourage more effort. However, based on many studies, the result appears to be the reverse: Praise, an extrinsic reward, crowds out the intrinsic satisfaction students experience from taking on a challenging task and completing it well. Therefore, it is better for teachers to praise students' effort and the strategies they used; these are aspects of performance that students can control. By responding in this manner, teachers show students that what is important is the quality of their thinking and the level of their effort.

Another manifestation of a teacher's response to students is the teacher's reaction to written assignments. Sometimes, because of lack of time or insufficient commitment to the work, students submit sloppy work or work of lower quality than the teacher knows they are capable of doing. By accepting inferior work, teachers send a signal to students that their expectations are low, that they don't believe the students are capable of achieving better results. Such a message is insidious and can undermine the teacher's other efforts to create an environment of high expectations and high cognitive challenge.

Rather than accepting inferior work, teachers send a powerful message to their students when they return the work and say something like "I know that you are capable of better work than this. Why don't you think this through again and hand it in tomorrow? Your grade on it won't be as high as it would have been if it had been up to your capability the first time, but it will be satisfactory and you'll have the satisfaction of completing a first-rate piece of work."

COMMENTARY ON THE INSTRUCTIONAL EXAMPLES

Both of the instructional examples provide illustrations of a safe and challenging environment. The tasks themselves are challenging, of course, and designed to engage students in thinking and reasoning. But beyond that, the ways in which teachers present and carry out these activities offer a positive and challenging environment for learning.

How Many Beans?

The question originally presented to students, "How many beans are in this jar?" is inherently intriguing. Most people confronted with a jar of beans would ask themselves that question. When students hazard an initial guess, teachers will notice that those estimates vary widely, sometimes by as much as a factor of 10.

Given the wide range of students' initial estimates, it's important that teachers accept all of them equally and refrain from giving any of the estimates greater credibility than any others. None should be rejected initially, and they should be recorded on the board with no names attached so that students don't later feel the need to defend their initial estimates. And students should not face ridicule from their classmates if they suggest an estimate that turns out to be completely off the mark.

As the unit moves on and students suggest methods for making a systematic estimate of the number of beans in the jar, the teacher's role in both challenging and supporting the learning becomes more complex. Of course, some of the support students receive will come from other students; because the students are working in small groups, the skills they have learned to support one another's efforts will pay dividends. That is, they will listen to one another's views and will refrain from using nonverbal behavior that suggests rejection or disdain.

The teacher's role during the small-group work is primarily one of facilitation and ongoing challenge. Student groups are working first to devise an approach to estimating the number of beans in the jar and then using the method they have selected. Teachers will find that certain students' efforts are in some way inadequate to the task: They will have skipped a step in their reasoning or they will make a serious error in computation and not recognize that the answer is unreasonable. It is in interacting with their students during this group work that teachers will convey both their expectations for high-level work and their support for their students as thinkers and learners.

One of the teacher's goals in these interactions is to encourage students' self-reliance and resilience, even in the face of challenges in the work itself. Another goal is to minimize students' dependence on the teacher's praise, which can transform an intrinsically interesting activity into one being completed only to earn positive comments. Intrinsic motivation to pursue the activity, in other words, may be transformed into extrinsic motivation for praise, thus undermining the students' self-confidence.

In a later phase of the unit, when the students make their presentations to the class regarding their group's approach and their findings, some teachers may again be challenged to offer support while insisting on work of high quality. If the teacher has worked with the small groups as they proceeded, none of the presentations will be obviously inadequate. But some will, no doubt, be superior to others; in encouraging student critiques of the work of their classmates, the teacher will help to ensure that students will find aspects of their peers' work to both admire and challenge. It is, of course, the *work*, and not the *students*, that is praised and challenged, and it is the safe environment that makes this distinction possible.

It is in the closure to the unit, when the teacher extracts from the class what they have collectively discovered, that the most important final learning occurs. That is, as a result of making their individual investigations and comparing them for accuracy and efficiency, the students will have discovered that some approaches are more efficient than others and that some give more accurate results than others. Students should be able to state in their own words why this is the case.

Pre-Revolutionary America

The initial worksheet for this unit, the "Signers of the Declaration of Independence," offers students an opportunity to make observations and to generate questions regarding the document and its place in a period of history. This is only the beginning, of course; it is the questions themselves, and the students' investigations of those questions, that form the heart of the unit.

Students must feel safe in offering questions about the worksheet; they should not be, and should know that they will not be, criticized by the teacher or ridiculed by their classmates as a result of their questions. Some questions will be mundane, such as "How many delegates attended from each colony?" whereas others will invite a deeper exploration of the period, such as "How were delegates selected (or were they elected, and if so by whom?) to attend?" In general, simpler questions will precede more complex ones; it is the teacher's role to ensure that questions at all levels are honored by the class.

When the students are settling on the questions they plan to investigate, the teacher's role is critical. The teacher will know, far better than the students, which questions are likely to yield interesting findings and which constitute a dead end. The teacher will also know which questions can be investigated, given the resources at the students' disposal. Thus, guidance at this stage is critical so that students will spend their time on an inquiry that yields interesting findings.

It's not only in steering students in interesting directions that the teacher plays an important role. Some students will deliberately choose an easy question, seeking to limit the amount of work required for the investigation. In these cases, the teacher's role is not to help students limit their question to one that can be answered given the time and the resources available; it is to urge them to challenge themselves, asking a more complex question than they might have chosen on their own.

Part of the reason for choosing an easy question may be that some students are not confident that they can perform a complex investigation. That is, they may be motivated not by the wish to make their life easier but instead to make it low-risk. A simpler question carries fewer risks than a more complex one; part of a teacher's role in challenging as well as supporting students is to convince them that they are capable of carrying out an investigation on a complex and interesting question.

While the students are working in groups to conduct their investigations, the teacher's role is again pivotal. There are many opportunities for students' efforts to go aground; for example, they may become discouraged or forget where they are in their inquiry. The teacher circulates, of course, and facilitates the work. But the teacher's role is not simply one of supporting and monitoring, although that too is necessary. It also includes pushing students when their efforts slacken and redirecting them when required.

When the student teams present their findings to the rest of the class, the teacher's role changes again. It may be necessary to remind students (and even to conduct a brief rehearsal of the process) that they must listen to their classmates respectfully and that a critical question does not imply criticism of the students themselves; it is a query about the students' findings or their methods of inquiry. And naturally, some presentations will be stronger than others. Part of the teacher's role is to ensure that the contributions of all groups are respected and honored for the effort they represent.

Finally, in structuring the closure to the unit, the teacher helps students consolidate their understanding of the pre–Revolutionary War period. Many important ideas and findings will have emerged from the student team reports; now it's vital for the teacher to help students know what they know, that is, how the findings from the different groups are related to one another. In reviewing the students' final essays, in which they summarize their findings in their own words, the teacher can ascertain the extent to which students have internalized the important concepts of the unit. This exercise serves both as a formative and a summative assessment, helping the teacher see how the learning of different students can be supported in the future.

Chapter 10

Management Matters

Some people, particularly noneducators, equate good classroom management with good teaching; an orderly class is regarded by some as the mark of an excellent teacher. It can be pointed out correctly that students can't learn anything in a chaotic atmosphere. Thus, classroom management skills contribute to the success of teachers, particularly those new to the profession. Of course, smooth management cannot replace good instruction; however, any lesson is more successful if engaging learning experiences are pursued in a well-run and organized classroom.

There are several components to successful classroom management, such as approaches to student conduct and policies for attendance and tardiness. Some of these are the result of policies established at the school (or in some cases even the district) level. (Grading, another important aspect of classroom culture, is addressed in Chapter 11, "Grading Student Performance.") Furthermore, issues of classroom management occur within a larger environment of respect and rapport; indeed, such an environment is a prerequisite for a smoothly running classroom.

The goal of all approaches to management matters is the same, namely, to create a classroom community that respects individuals and permits all voices to be heard. In particular, a teacher's approach to classroom management must ensure an orderly environment in which students are able to learn. They must not fear chaos or inequitable treatment of individuals; they must be able to focus on the activities of the class without apprehension that they will be surrounded by mayhem. However, although the goal of teachers' policies and practices toward classroom management is to ensure a smoothly running classroom, this does not imply that teachers' methods must be dictatorial. In fact, in this area, no less than in the design of instruction, it's important to bear in mind what we know about learning and motivation in order to enlist students' own energies. It is also helpful to consider what we have already learned about our students and apply this knowledge to building respect and rapport both between the teacher and students and among the students.

AN ENVIRONMENT OF RESPECT AND RAPPORT

Everything in the classroom happens within the environment of the class; it is the way they were treated that people recall years later when thinking about their school experiences. Thus, if teachers want to create a purposeful, organized classroom environment, it must be within the context of the relationships that have been built there.

An environment of respect is primarily a matter of interactions, both between the teacher and students and among the students. When teachers succeed in securing student cooperation in the classroom, it is because students feel safe there. They know that they will not be ridiculed, undermined, or demeaned.

In creating a positive atmosphere, tone is everything. Teachers have far more power than students, but experienced teachers don't rely on that power to maintain order in the classroom. Rather, they enlist the cooperation of students by honoring them, by demonstrating that they care about them, by taking an interest in them as people, including their backgrounds, interests, and activities outside the classroom. When they speak to students, they do so politely, using such statements as "Ladies and gentlemen, could we get underway?"

What we know about learning and student motivation is relevant to classroom management. It's important for students, like all people, to feel that they have some choice and control over their lives; hence, they are far more likely to make a commitment to classroom rules and procedures if they have contributed to them.

This choice and control cannot be contrived; when teachers invite students to contribute their ideas to matters of management, it's important that students not get the impression that their role is merely to "come up with" what the teacher had in mind anyway. Their ideas must actually be reflected in the final product. There is a role for teacher facilitation, to be sure; the teacher might collect a number of student ideas for procedures for group work, for example, and then help students organize those ideas under a few broad categories. But the student contributions must be honored and used in a manner that makes it clear to students that they have played an important role.

The subject of interactions can itself be a topic for student discussion and consensus. How do students want to be treated by the teacher and by other students? When asked, students will report that they want to be treated well, not made to feel embarrassed, and so on. But the important part of such conversations occurs when the teacher invites students to describe how they would recognize respect or lack of respect from their classmates. What would a classmate say or do that would make them feel respected or insulted? By articulating these behaviors in the abstract, it's possible to call attention to them when they occur as illustrating the points that were made earlier.

All the other aspects of classroom management are more easily addressed if teachers have spent time initially with their classes in creating an environment of respect. The form of such conversations varies, naturally, with the age of the students. But even young children have views on this important topic; those views should be respected.

CLASSROOM ROUTINES

The aim of all classroom routines is the same: an efficient and smoothly running classroom to maximize the time available for learning. There are many different elements of classroom routines: distribution of materials, transitions to different groups, and so on, and they all contribute to either a chaotic or a seamless operation.

Attention Signal

The first, and in some respects the most important, aspect of classroom routines is the teacher's ability to call a class to order. This might be at the beginning of a lesson, after a transition between activities, or between an individual and a small-group activity. Some teachers flash the lights and others use a gentle bell, but the objective is the same: for students to redirect their attention to the teacher so that the lesson can proceed. If students are working quietly, it may not be necessary to use a specific technique; simply speaking may attract their attention. Of course, when teachers ask for students' attention, they should be alert to the possibility that they are interrupting students in their work. For that reason it should be done with respect, using a comment such as "When you've finished your sentence, could you please direct your attention here?"

Fear of losing control of students' attention causes some teachers to refuse to allow group work or individual activities. They fear that once they have "turned the students loose," they will never be able to get them back. Such fears are understandable, of course, particularly among inexperienced teachers. Fortunately, they are also unfounded;

routines for calling the class to attention are skills, and like other skills, they can be taught to students.

Like many aspects of classroom management, procedures are best taught to students as specific examples of a general principle: "There are a lot of people in this class; we must make the best possible use of our time; people can't learn if they can't hear the teacher or one another. So, when students have been doing one thing (such as small-group work), what can we agree would be a good technique to get students' attention? What should be the guidelines as to how the signal will work? That is, should the signal result in instantaneous silence? Should students be permitted to complete the sentence they are speaking? Should the signal be, in effect, a thirty-second warning?" The answers to these questions matter, since lack of consensus on them can result in little more order than having no guidelines at all.

Once the guidelines have been established, they should be practiced so that students feel comfortable with them. Hence, following the discussion establishing guidelines, while students are engaged in group work, the teacher might call them to attention, not because she or he wants to shift the focus of the lesson, but only to practice the routine. Then, following a brief review of the students' success in carrying out the routine, they can resume their previous work. The purpose at the outset, then, is not to use the routine to promote learning but to establish and practice the routine itself. Procedures are then, from time to time, reviewed and reinforced so that students do not forget them or feel that they are no longer important.

Distributing and Collecting Materials

A teacher's skill in organizing teaching materials is an important mark of his or her management skills. In fact, one reason some teachers are reluctant to use physical materials is their fear that, for example, math and science manipulative materials will become projectiles that students hurl across the room. Or, less dramatically, they may anticipate chaos as they try to distribute or collect papers for a written activity.

As with the attention signal, the goal of routines for distribution and collection of materials is to maximize the time available for student learning; hence, efficiency is the key. The details of the procedures vary, naturally, with the age of the students and the type of material being handled: worksheets may be put on tables for the students themselves to hand around to everyone there; for distributing markers or other physical materials, one person from each small group can collect them for the group.

And, like other routines, the distribution and collection of materials can be practiced. At first, this will take a little time as the teacher reminds the students, before giving the signal to proceed, of the agreed-upon procedures. Then, following the distribution or collection, it is sensible to refocus the attention of the class on the routine itself: How successful was it? Could it be improved? Some teachers even keep track of the time needed for this routine, using a stopwatch and recording the time on the board. This gives the students a vivid record of how they are improving in their performance of the routine.

Managing Instructional Groups

Two of the disincentives for some teachers to use small-group work in their teaching are the fear that students will not work productively when they are not directly engaged with the teacher or the fear of chaos as students move from one type of group to another. Of course, there are many advantages to small-group work: Students enjoy it; they can interact with their friends, thus satisfying their need for connections with others. Some students, who out of shyness or insecurity might not volunteer an opinion in the large group, may be more inclined to participate in a small group discussion. Teachers can provide, if appropriate, different assignments for various groups of students. Furthermore, small-group work provides opportunities for students to acquire important collaborative skills, which is essential for their future success in both work and further education.

But group work definitely carries risks. Inevitably, some students are not under direct supervision while the teacher is working with other groups. And students typically move from group to group or between full-class and small-group work. If these procedures are not well established, either chaos or loss of valuable time may result.

Again, teachers must be direct and forthright with students about their procedures. Students can understand the issues: They are working, for example, in small groups solving a problem or undertaking an investigation. The teacher can be in only one part of the classroom at any given time. So, students must have an orderly procedure for signaling that they require the teacher's attention. Alternatively, they can be taught to first seek the assistance of classmates for either an individual assignment or the work of a small group. Or they can learn to skip over the parts of the assignment on which they need help, continuing to work on the parts that they can do independently.

The same thinking applies to moving from one group to another; if students understand the need for an orderly process in shifting from one grouping pattern to another, they can suggest ways of making that happen efficiently. When the procedure has been decided upon and practiced a few times, a simple signal on the part of the teacher will tell students that they should use it.

Performing Noninstructional Duties

There are few marks of experience as telling as a teacher's skill in performing noninstructional duties, from taking attendance, to collecting lunch money, to doing a quick check to determine which students have completed their homework assignment for the day. An experienced teacher can accomplish these tasks in a few seconds, whereas a new teacher might require 5 to 10 minutes. Again, enlisting student assistance is vital; young children enjoy the responsibility of taking attendance or of "signing themselves in" on a daily chart. Older students can take over many of these jobs and even suggest efficient approaches to them. The aim is, of course, the same: to spend as little instructional time as possible. In fact, experienced teachers frequently organize the procedures for noninstructional duties such that students are engaged in an activity while they do it, thereby spending no instructional time on them at all. For example, in a math class, students might know that they are to begin work on a problem written on the board while the teacher takes attendance at the beginning of a class period.

Another aspect of noninstructional tasks concerns procedures for such things as students sharpening their pencils or going to the washroom. Again, it's important to establish these routines at the beginning of a school year so that they are not "negotiated" every day or even every week, diverting energy from the important work of learning.

Managing Traffic Flow

Another important aspect of classroom life is traffic flow. Most classrooms are rather crowded places, and it's important for students not to collide with one another as they move about. Spaces between desks or groups of desks must be sufficient to allow free movement. Equally important, students must understand the value of common courtesy as the go from one part of the classroom to another.

As with other classroom routines, students themselves will have suggestions for how to organize the classroom to provide the maximum freedom and efficiency of movement. And when problems arise—when students get "bunched up" while getting art supplies, for example, or when they run into one another on their way to the door—they can suggest an improvement in traffic flow.

Teachers must also be able to move easily around the classroom as they monitor student learning and behavior. Being able to move quickly and quietly to one area of the classroom to intervene before a potential misbehavior occurs is important. Calling out to a student from across the room only serves to pull other students off task, but quickly moving to the potential problem can redirect the potential misbehavior before it escalates.

Keeping sufficient room between the rows and having students place backpacks and supplies for other classes out of the way are just two examples of how teachers improve not only the students' ability to move around the classroom, but also their own.

STUDENT CONDUCT

Classrooms are crowded places, and students greatly outnumber teachers. Teachers, particularly those just entering the profession, worry that their students won't accept their authority, willfully disregarding class rules or the teacher's directions. They may be haunted by the prospect of defiant students disobeying them and, as an added insult, mocking them.

In general, such fears are misguided; powerful norms regarding teachers' authority are well established. When young children "play school," their version of school is frequently authoritarian and even punitive. It's interesting to observe, and one wonders where such ideas of school originate; this type of play may be observed even in very young preschool children.

The general purpose of classroom standards of student conduct is straightforward: to ensure an orderly environment for learning. But there are many issues related to student conduct that are worth exploring.

Public Standards of Conduct

Like most aspects of life in schools, standards of conduct for students should be well known and public. There is no place for mystery: Students should know the rules with which they are expected to comply. Indeed, many teachers find that if the students themselves help create the rules, they are more likely to obey them and to play an active role in encouraging their classmates to comply.

Number of Rules and Level of Detail

Some teachers are tempted to create (either on their own or with the assistance of their students) many rules to cover every conceivable situation that might arise. Other teachers, opting for simplicity, create only a few rules, which are stated, of necessity, in rather general terms. In general, simplicity is preferable, because it is impossible to anticipate every possible situation for which a rule might be needed. Furthermore, if only a few rules are created, they may be seen as general principles from which specific guidelines are derived. For example, if the rule is to "respect other students," then that would mean not interrupting classmates during a discussion, not passing stories about classmates, and so on.

Creating Classroom Rules

Many teachers find that they can have an important and interesting conversation with their students regarding how students should behave in class. Of course, the conversation will vary, depending on the age of the students, but regardless of their age, students can play an active role in creating the rules for their classroom.

A procedure that works well for these conversations consists of inviting students to contribute ideas to a class list on the conditions that allow them to do their best work. They mention things such as "quiet enough to concentrate," "I'm able to find supplies when I need them," or "classmates don't make me feel bad when I need to ask for help." These ideas can then be clustered under some general categories that, depending on the students' age, they may be able to generate. Such categories might be "How we treat one another" and "How we create an atmosphere for learning." Then students can generate specific examples of how they should treat one another, which reflect, of course, how they want to be treated by others. The examples will be age appropriate, but will range from situations in class to those on the playground, during class assignments and in moving around the room.

An advantage of this approach is that when a new situation arises, the teacher does not have to create a new rule to address it. Instead, the teacher can simply ask the students, "What of our class rules addresses this situation?"

All in all, standards of conduct (in other words, behavior management) are best specified by a few general principles that govern a wide range of situations. And when students themselves help to create these standards, they are far more likely to accept them than if the rules seem to be imposed from above. Classroom communities created by the students themselves give students a sense of power and autonomy; their classrooms are, after all, important aspects of their lives, and when they help create the environment, they are exercising an important aspect of freedom and choice.

Monitoring Student Behavior

Effective teachers do indeed seem to have eyes in the back of their heads. They are continuously aware of what is going on in their classroom. Jacob Kounin (1977) called it *withitness*. Teachers do this by scanning the class and looking for potential problems, walking around the room and spending time in each quarter, making eye contact with students, and giving them nonverbal signals in order to redirect them without distracting the other students.

Interventions in inappropriate student behavior must maintain the dignity of the students, help them refocus on their work, and promote better behavior in the future.

ATTENDANCE AND TARDINESS

Most schools have policies concerning attendance and tardiness; some of these policies are quite elaborate and can result in students receiving a failing grade in a course if they miss more than, for example, 18 school days during a year.

But in addition, teachers establish their own policies regarding attendance and tardiness. How should they respond, for example, if a student is habitually late for class or if an extended absence results in a major assignment being turned in late? What principles should guide a teacher's approach to such situations?

Age of the Students

Issues of attendance and tardiness differ profoundly, depending on whether students are in elementary or high school. With young children, it's fair to assume that if school is relatively rewarding and supportive, they would rather be in class than at home. That is, after all, where their friends are, and it's likely to be fun. Similarly, if young children are late for school or miss the bus, it's probable that their parents are not sufficiently organized to make sure that they get there on time.

However, as children grow older, they are able to assume greater responsibility for both attendance and punctuality. They can take charge of organizing their materials for school, setting an alarm, and boarding the bus. This is not easy, of course, although such efforts provide an opportunity for important learning. However, teachers must recognize that the age of students makes a difference when thinking about attendance and tardiness, and they must respond accordingly. If the problem, in other words, rests with parents rather than students, a rigid policy applied to students is unlikely to have the desired result.

Flexibility

The first rule for teachers in regard to students' attendance in class must be flexibility. Context matters. Situations are fluid. When a student must dash through the halls of a crowded high school and realizes en route that something must be retrieved from a locker, arriving late is virtually inevitable.

Issues of tardiness during the school day, and related issues of the school schedule and the time permitted between classes, are best addressed on a schoolwide basis. But when, on occasion, a student comes dashing in late to class after an unplanned stop at a locker or when a student's illness prevents the on-time completion of a major project, flexibility is important. After all, a teacher has no interest in destroying a student's enthusiasm for learning, and rigid application of a rule is likely to make students cynical and negative toward school. On the other hand, when teachers demonstrate that they are willing to help students complete their work and demonstrate high-level learning (even if they must be somewhat inconsistent in dealing with various students), the students themselves appreciate this flexibility.

However, teachers must be alert to the possibility that some students will take advantage of a teacher whom they consider soft and try to "game" the system. To counter this possibility, teachers must be alert for patterns and, when necessary, take a student aside to discuss the situation and to determine, together with the student, a way forward. There are two important principles at work here, and they may occasionally be in conflict. One is the principle of fairness; students should have reason to believe that teachers are even-handed in their application of important classroom rules. The other principle is flexibility. Students should know that their teachers will, if the occasion demands it, be responsive to unforeseen situations as they arise. It might be helpful to remember that fairness does not equate with "one size (or rule) fits all"; situations and students are different in ways that make a difference in enforcing the rules.

Summary

Issues of classroom management are significant in setting the tone for a class. Particularly for new teachers, management procedures are important to establish as part of setting and maintaining the relationships between teacher and students and among students. Classroom management is not an afterthought; it can benefit from the same high-quality thinking and planning as other aspects of an instructional program. Management matters are not the raison d'être of teaching, but they make a significant contribution to the success of any approach to instruction. They provide the space for good instruction to occur; they create an orderly environment so that the students and teacher can get on with the important work of the classroom.

Chapter 11

Grading Student Performance

More than any other practice, the manner in which students are graded reflects the school's approach to students and their learning. For example, does the school grade on a curve? What's the highest grade that can be awarded for work turned in late? If students score poorly on a test, can they retake it? If so, what is the highest grade they can receive? In answering these questions, a school's faculty must address a number of important issues.

In some schools, the grading policy is established by the school or the district, with all teachers following similar procedures. The teachers must simply implement the official policy. Other schools give considerable latitude to teachers, allowing them to develop their own approach. In any event, many teachers have their own philosophy about grading that they can incorporate into their grading practices, even if these are part of a larger school or district policy.

Grading student performance is a complex matter, particularly at the high school level. And grading is notoriously inconsistent; the same essay may receive an A from one teacher and a C from another. Teachers, in other words, tend to apply their own standards of quality when looking at student work, standards that are rarely communicated either to students or to other teachers. When such idiosyncratic standards are used, grading becomes a high-stakes affair that can adversely affect students' future.

This chapter explores the important concepts about grading student performance. It also invites teachers to consider their own practices in light of what we know about students and their learning.

MEANING OF GRADES

Before embarking on a general discussion of the purposes and practices of grading, it's important to consider what grades mean. We refer to someone as an "A student." What do we mean by that? That the student is especially intelligent or works really hard or is very good in, for example, mathematics? What does a C mean? Does it mean that the quality of a student's work represents the average for all students in the class? Or does it mean that the student has fulfilled all the requirements for the class but has not excelled in them? Does it mean that a student is prepared to take the next course in the sequence, proceeding, for example, from French I to French II?

Most of the discussions in which teachers engage about grading (and they are frequently heated) center on the meaning of grades. Because many schools are organized around a behaviorist, extrinsic-motivation view of students and their learning, it is assumed that grades (or, in elementary schools, gold stars) can be used to motivate students to work hard and that they would not do so in the absence of grades. Therefore, many teachers incorporate issues such as attitude, completion of homework, and the like into their calculations of grades.

On the other hand, when teachers take a more constructivist view of learning and motivation, their attitudes toward grading must shift. When teachers understand that intrinsic motivation is more powerful and enduring than extrinsic motivation, they must structure their approach to grading to reflect what we know about students' drive for mastery of important learning. In addition, teachers must consider how their approach to grading will motivate students to take charge of their own learning.

Before moving to recommendations about grading, it is useful to understand some of the enduring beliefs about the subject. Below are some of the factors that many teachers consider in determining the grades they award.

Difficulty of the Material

Some teachers appear to believe that the grades they award reflect the level of challenge of the content; high school teachers of advanced science courses have been heard to brag that they "never give A's," as though the paucity of high-level student achievement is a consequence of the difficulty of the course. The lower the grades, in other words, the higher the teacher's standards.

This position is difficult to justify: In what other profession would low levels of achievement of the stated outcomes constitute evidence of professional skill? We would not think more highly of physicians with high levels of patient mortality, nor would large numbers of airline crashes support claims of skill by aeronautical engineers. If a teacher's primary responsibility is to advance student learning, then surely the evidence of a teacher's skill is in the demonstrated learning, not failure of that teacher's students on measures of achievement. It is only a reverse sense of professional rigor that encourages a teacher to brag: "I have such high standards that virtually no student ever receives an A."

Effort

Some teachers believe that the amount of effort expended by students should determine (or at least contribute to) their grade. This appears to be particularly the case when students seem to have no natural aptitude for a subject but, through hard work, manage to achieve a certain level of skill. "He worked so *hard;* how can that be worth only a B?" is a commonly heard expression of this point of view.

Completion of Assignments

Other teachers award "points" and then grades based on whether students actually complete homework and class assignments. They care less about the quality of the student work, or whether the work reflects student understanding of the material, than about the fact that the students did the assignments.

Basing grades on the completion of assignments is a variation on the theme of basing grades on student effort; such completion reflects the student's commitment to the course and a willingness to devote time to fulfilling its requirements. Surely this commitment and this willingness to spend time should be rewarded!

Undeniably, it's important for students to come to class prepared—to have read the assigned literature, for example, or to have completed the writing assignment so that students can engage in self or peer editing. And if students are not sufficiently engaged in the work to complete their assignments without prodding, some system of rewards may be necessary. In meeting this challenge, some teachers designate a portion of the grade (small but not insignificant, such as 20%) to various measures of preparation and participation. This includes not only coming to class prepared, but also the level of engagement in class activities and discussions.

However, if students are required by the grading system to demonstrate completion of homework assignments, those assignments must be of high quality; it makes no sense for students to be railroaded into completing assignments that are, for them, simply busywork. This issue is addressed more fully in Chapter 8, "Designing Learning Experiences."

Progress

All teachers know that any class contains students whose past performance in a subject has been poor; when such students demonstrate remarkable improvement over the course of a school year, their teachers are tempted to recognize such improvement with a higher grade than they might award to students who began the year at a more proficient level. Thus, teachers observing dramatic improvement from, for example D-quality to B-quality work by the end of the year may be tempted to award a grade of B for the entire year, ignoring the lower quality of earlier work. This practice may reward students for their hard work and progress, but it could be challenged by other students on the grounds of equity.

Performance of Other Students

Some schools have a policy of grading "on a curve," meaning that a certain percentage of students (and no more) are awarded an A, another percentage a B, and so forth. Although largely discredited, this practice persists in some schools. It is justified as a way of maintaining high standards; however, the consequences of grading on a curve are widespread and pernicious.

- Even if all students in a class perform at a very high level, grading on a curve would require that some students receive a failing grade.
- Some schools may attempt to circumvent this requirement by applying the curve not to each class but to all students in, say, the 10th grade.
- In a school with a policy of grading on a curve, some students, typically those with a history of difficulty in school, may decide that their chances of ever receiving high grades, regardless of their effort, are slim.
- When students are compared to one another and graded accordingly, they are less likely to cooperate with their classmates or to offer assistance to struggling peers.
- Some students may be reluctant to enroll in challenging courses, fearing that they will not be able to perform as well as others in the class.

All in all, the practice of grading on a curve has only negative consequences and should be avoided.

Mastery of the Curriculum

In some schools, grades are based on how well students demonstrate that they have achieved the outcomes established in the curriculum. Thus, for example, if a student masters 82% of the objectives of a unit, the grade awarded would be 82 or its letter equivalent.

There are numerous practical difficulties with grading students solely on the basis of their achievement in the curriculum; these are considered below. However, the principle is solid; students' grades should reflect their performance in the course in which they are enrolled and should not be "contaminated" by other factors such as their natural ability in the subject or the performance of other students.

PURPOSES OF GRADING

Grading serves several purposes, and some of these, unfortunately, are in conflict with one another. It must be recognized, however, that the purposes of grading are fundamentally different in elementary and high school, with middle school somewhere in between.

Communicating with Parents

Particularly for elementary students, the primary purpose of grading, as manifested in the report card, is to show parents how well their children are progressing. Most parents are not interested in detailed communication; they do not care whether their child can solve two-step as opposed to one-step word problems. What they mostly want to know is whether their child is "on track," not falling behind in, for example, third grade. They want reassurance that their child is "okay."

Of course, the best communication with parents is through personal contact. A report card, after all, cannot convey everything that parents are legitimately concerned about. They may want to know whether their daughter chooses to read in school, whether she is loyal to her friends, or whether their son perseveres in the face of initial difficulty in understanding. Comments on report cards can communicate some of these matters, but they tend to be brief and may appear "canned" and impersonal to parents.

In some schools, typically those with relatively small class sizes and primarily at the elementary level, teachers write detailed narrative reports to parents about their children's progress. Although very time-consuming, these reports are appreciated by parents, and they can convey a far wider range of perspectives on a child's learning than is possible through a "checklist" report card.

Communicating with Students

Grades, and the process of deriving grades, can provide a mechanism for communicating with students about what is important and how they are measuring up on the important outcomes in a unit or course. For example, when math teachers include, as part of their grades, students' reasoning strategies used to solve problems, students realize that it's not only the right answer that counts. And when students receive a grade on their skill in working with classmates, they learn that collaborative skills are as important as conceptual understanding.

Naturally, in order for grades to be useful in informing students about the teacher's learning objectives, those objectives and their methods of assessment must be made explicit. As in everything else dealing with assessment, a teacher's criteria for grading and the expected standards of performance should not be a secret. And as described in Chapter 7, "Assessing Student Learning," the criteria, standards, and rubrics should, to the extent possible, be created with input from the students themselves.

Motivating Students

There is no doubt that, at least with some students, the prospect of high grades has a motivating effect. It is one of the realities of high school life that if students want to attend a selective college, they must demonstrate their readiness through their record, which in most cases includes high grades.

It is certainly the case that intrinsic motivation is, generally speaking, a more powerful motivator than extrinsic motivation. Furthermore, extrinsic motivation tends to "drive out" intrinsic motivation. (See Chapter 4, "What We Know About Motivation," for a full discussion of this subject.) However, extrinsic motivation, in the form of the prospect of a high grade, does encourage students to devote the time and focused energy needed to master difficult content.

However, teachers should also remember that it's important for students to recognize high grades as evidence of learning and competence, not as a reward for "jumping through hoops." That is, when students devote energy to mastering difficult content, the high grade they receive on a test or an assignment constitutes important validation that they have indeed mastered that content. It is highly satisfying for a student to be able to go into a test with the confidence to say, "Ask me anything!" Such a feeling represents a sense of competence and power, also an important motivator. Thus, although the grades themselves may motivate students to work hard, the feeling of satisfaction that accompanies the belief in one's own control over difficult material is also extremely rewarding.

In some schools and with some students, conversations about grades boil down to questions such as "What do I have to do to get a B?" or "Could I do something for extra credit to get a higher grade?" Such questions reflect the attitude among students, and perhaps that of their teachers, that grades represent what students *do,* not what they *learn.* It also reflects the idea, prevalent in some schools, that grades represent an area of negotiation between students and teacher.

Communicating with Other Educators

Grades, in many schools, are an important component of communication between educators, either directly or indirectly. For example, a grade of B in Spanish I signals to other teachers in the Modern Languages department that a student is prepared to learn Spanish II. This use of grades is important in those fields in which prerequisites play an important role, particularly mathematics and world languages.

This application of the grading system is one more reason why it's important for grades to reflect the level of students' mastery of the curriculum. If grades demonstrate, for example, a student's standing compared with other students or a reward for hard work, the teacher in, for example, Spanish II has no way of knowing whether a student is prepared for her course.

Of course, there are other mechanisms that are even better suited to communication between educators than grades; grades are, after all, a fairly blunt instrument. When they inherit students from a teacher in another course, it's helpful for teachers to know the students' strengths and weaknesses in the curriculum. For example, a student might be highly proficient in speaking Spanish but far less so in reading the language. A simple grade of B would not convey these nuances, which are very important for the teacher of Spanish II. Thus, a more nuanced method of communicating between educators, especially if they are in the same school, should be devised, such as more detailed enumerations of the content of a course and each student's level of proficiency in each segment.

Communicating with the Outside World

Good grades are important for students seeking admission to colleges, universities, and technical schools; directors of admissions regard high school grades as the primary predictor of whether students are prepared for the rigors of more advanced schooling. Indeed, grades in high school are a good predictor of grades in college, particularly when supplemented by other information, such as scores on college admissions tests and personal interviews.

Employers also look at a student's transcript for clues to the academic achievements of individuals they are considering hiring. It's important to note, however, that many employers are interested in qualities that may be only indirectly reflected in students' high school grades, such as their punctuality, their honesty and integrity, and their aptitude for learning new skills.

ISSUES IN GRADING

All adults in the course of their own schooling have had experience with grading. Sometimes it seemed fair, at other times not. Many people recall times from their school and college days when they "got away with" not studying. That is, they were lucky on a test; it focused on the things they happened to know. In other instances, though, a test, or the entire grading system of which it is a part, feels very unfair to current students. If students receive grades based on their competence in a course, and if the teacher has succeeded in teaching so that every student learns well, then the result will be large numbers of students with grades of A or B. This result is very different from the situation that exists in most schools today; its consequences have to be carefully thought through.

There are a number of issues dealing with grading; these are addressed below.

Selecting and Sorting

Traditionally, the role of grades has been to determine, through 12 years of schooling, which students were suited to attend 4-year colleges and which were more suited for community colleges, technical colleges, or movement directly into the workforce. This has been a consequence of grading on a curve because the number of high grades is limited. And if the number is limited, only the most qualified receive them.

Not only have many people expected schools to select, through their grading practices, those students most likely to succeed in college, but also there has been great stability over time in the way students are grouped for instruction. Thus, the "bluebird" reading group in second grade translates, 10 years later, into the AP English course. And when one considers that students' reading level in lower elementary grades is largely determined by their socioeconomic status, it's easy to see how the nation's educational and economic stratification persists over time.

Grade Inflation

When schools are organized for high-level student learning and when teachers engage virtually all students successfully, most students learn well. And when students' grades are based on their success in learning, it's possible that there will be many A's in a class. Some might regard this as grade inflation. It is not. Instead, it is standards-based grading, in which students' grades reflect the level of their learning.

Some teachers resist this approach. In fact, a teacher in upstate New York commented that "I could do this. I could teach well, so that every student did work at the level of an A or a B. In fact, I could imagine our entire department doing this. Suppose every student in our classes learned science at a high level? Suppose every department in the school did it, and every student in the school made A's and B's in every course? How would Cornell know who to pick?"

This remark is revealing. Teachers have for so long accepted responsibility for using the grading system to indicate which students are suited for selective colleges that the concept that grades might reflect high-level learning is quite alien. But a response to that teacher is "That's a serious problem, isn't it? But actually, that's not our problem; it's Cornell's problem. And wouldn't you love to give Cornell that problem?"

Thus, grade inflation itself does not present a problem for schools or the larger society. In fact, if the grades awarded reflect what students have learned, it's not inflation at all. What presents problems for schools and for the larger society is the belief that the role of schools is not to teach all students at high levels, but rather to determine (based on questionable criteria) which students should be admitted to selective colleges.

RECOMMENDATIONS

Given all the factors discussed above, how should teachers grade students? The following recommendations attempt to craft a grading policy based on student learning while using what is known about how students learn and how they are motivated. A distinction should be made between grading policies for elementary and secondary students. In general, elementary teachers don't have to contend with the knowledge that their grades will influence students' prospects for college admission.

Elementary Students

The primary purpose of grading at the elementary level is to communicate with parents. Parents need assurance that their children are making adequate progress so that they can respond if additional help is needed. A secondary purpose of grading at the elementary level is to convey information to other teachers, although most schools have other, and better, methods for doing this.

Therefore, recommended procedures for grading at the elementary level are those that offer information to parents and an indication of their child's progress. For example, the system should tell parents that their child is making satisfactory progress in the third-grade math (and reading, and social studies) curriculum.

Of course, if the recommendations presented in Chapter 10, "Management Matters," have been followed, then parents will have been kept abreast of their children's daily work through assignments done at home. Furthermore, if students and parents participate together in student-led conferences, the formal report card is supplemented by a conversation that is far richer and more nuanced than anything that can be communicated through simple grades.

An elementary school report card should tell parents how the student is progressing in the standard curriculum and provide information about other issues, such as the child's effort, progress, and participation in class or his or her skills in working with and respecting classmates. But letter grades serve no useful purpose. For example, a report card might indicate that a student is working at an advanced level in an area of the curriculum, such as reading (reading books at the fourth-grade level in third grade, for instance). It could also indicate that this same student does not make much effort in class, relying on his past proficiency to enable him to coast in school. Alternatively, a student might be working at a lower level in the curriculum, still struggling to master concepts in the second-grade math curriculum, for example, while enrolled in the third grade but making a strong effort and being well liked by his classmates.

Providing parents with a realistic assessment of their children's progress is important; parents don't appreciate the shock of having been told for several years that the student is "making good progress," only to discover later that during all that time the student, although working hard, was performing significantly below the level of his or her classmates. When honestly told the actual situation, some parents may provide additional assistance or summer school enrollment to help their child catch up to his or her peers. Such additional help should not be seen as punitive; it is simply a response to a situation.

Alternatively, additional assistance may be provided through the school as part of its program of *learning support,* either during school hours or after school. Parents, if they are kept apprised of their children's progress, will appreciate the benefit of such assistance and can discuss it with their children in a positive light.

Secondary Students

The recommended grading procedures for secondary students are more complex than those for elementary students for the simple reason that the situation is more complex. Grades serve a broader array of purposes; they have a number of different audiences, and the realities of grades' impact on student motivation and effort must be weighed.

THE TRADITIONAL "BARGAIN"   Many new teachers of high school students are surprised to encounter the belief among some students that they can strike a "bargain" with their teachers over the issue of grading. With some students, the first question they have with respect to a teacher's grading policy is some variation on "What do I have to do to get an A (or a B)?" Alternatively, toward the end of a marking period, when students realize that their grade, as calculated by the teacher's formula, is likely to be a "B" will ask, "Can I do some extra work to bring this up to an A?" In both cases, students equate the grades they receive not with the quality of their understanding but with the amount of effort they are willing to expend. They then reserve the option of deciding whether the effort they would have to make for the higher grade is "worth it."

These students, with their teachers' willing participation, regard grading as a deal to be negotiated between students and teachers in which they are both expected to uphold their end; the students make a certain amount of effort, and the teacher gives them a certain grade.

In some schools, this bargain has an even less productive subtext; the deal includes some assurance on the part of students that they won't make life too hard on the teacher if the teacher does not demand too much of them. That is, in some settings, students decide that, due to their larger physical size, or their general disrespect for the school and the values of rigor and sustained effort that it represents, they will cooperate with the teacher only if he or she does not make too many demands and gives them acceptable grades. The teacher's bargain amounts to "If you don't make too much trouble and if you are minimally compliant in this class, you will receive at least a C (or some other grade)." In other words, the grades represent nothing more than a bargaining chip that teachers can use to "buy" compliance in class.

This incidence of such a bargain should not be overestimated. In most schools, students accept the school's culture of high-level learning and the intellectual elbow grease that such learning requires. But in many schools, at least some students attempt to make a deal with the teacher, negotiating for a higher grade.

Of course, there is a fundamental difference between a student asking "What do I have to do to move my grade from a B to an A?" and a student asking "How can I improve my writing (for example) so that it meets the standards of A-quality performance?" The first student is asking what she should *do* (what extra-credit assignment is available); the second student is asking what she should *learn* in order to demonstrate writing of a higher quality. The first is asking to make a deal; the second is asking for feedback. These are fundamentally different attitudes on the part of students, although teachers may require experience to be able to discern the difference.

A BETTER BARGAIN   Of course, even teachers in standards-based schools committed to high-level learning make a bargain of sorts with their students. It goes something like this: The teacher says, in effect, "If we all do what we should do, I can guarantee you a good grade in this course. That is, I'll be as good a teacher as I can; I'll give interesting assignments, I'll provide explanations that are as clear as possible; I'll give you opportunities to develop your understanding; I'll be available for extra assistance before or after school or at other times during the school day. But you have to do your part as well: You must come to class prepared and ready to work; you must be alert for those times when you do not understand something; you have to be willing to come for extra assistance if you need it. In other words, you must make a commitment to high-quality learning. If you do that, I guarantee that you will do well."

There is a subtext to this bargain. The teacher is not only offering a deal to students; he or she is expressing confidence that the students are capable of high-level learning if they are willing to work hard. That is a powerful message to students and contributes greatly to their sense of their own intelligence and capability. They are also hearing that they will be able to master difficult content; this is a powerful and highly motivating message.

There is a second subtext to this bargain as well: The teacher is expressing confidence that he or she is skilled enough to help any student who makes the commitment to learning achieve good results. Not every teacher has such confidence; teachers must be willing to risk their own vulnerabilities. This confidence is a consequence of expertise and of teachers' experience with success. Some teachers, until they acquire such experience, find it difficult to make a commitment of success to their students.

However, when teachers are willing to take such risks, the results are powerful; the teacher and students become, in effect, partners in the students' learning. The teacher's role changes from that of judge and jury over the students' futures to one of coach in helping students achieve at a high level. Thus, the teacher is saying, in effect, "My job is to help you succeed. You must help in that process; you must work hard and monitor your own learning. My job is not to judge you but rather to help you achieve the high standards that we have set for this course." Of course, teachers who have taught AP or IB courses, or even have worked to help students prepare for the GED exam, are familiar with this dynamic. The standard is an external one, and the teacher's role is to help students meet that standard. These same conditions can prevail in a normal classroom.

THE GOLD STANDARD OF GRADING   Many schools adopt a schoolwide grading policy to which all teachers must adhere. But if teachers have flexibility in implementing it, the following principles would constitute a gold standard of grading. Alternatively, teachers might work to convince their colleagues of the value of such an approach.

- *A Certain Percentage of Students' Grades Designated for "Preparation and Participation."*   For a class to be successful, it's essential that students come to class prepared to participate and that they do indeed take part in instructional activities and discussions. To that end, teachers count that aspect of student performance as some previously announced percentage of students' grades, such as 20%.
- *Assessments Aligned with Instructional Outcomes.*   As described in Chapter 7, "Assessing Student Learning," teachers devise assessments so that they know the extent to which their students have achieved the learning specified in their outcome statements. These assessments will include tests, written work, observations of student performance, and the like.
- *Student Learning Assessed on Each Instructional Unit, Using the Assessments.*   Using the assessments designed for the range of instructional outcomes, teachers assess student learning and evaluate that learning against their required standards of performance.
- *Students' Grades Calculated for Each Unit According to the Assessments and Established Standards.*   Based on student performance on the assessments, teachers determine whether students have achieved at the required standard of performance for the unit. If they have done so, their grade for the unit is at least a B.
- *Awarding a Grade of "Incomplete" to Students Whose Level of Performance Is Not Yet Up to the Required Standard.*   The grade of Incomplete tells students that they have not yet mastered the required content, but that the teacher believes they are capable of doing so and is prepared to provide whatever assistance is needed to ensure success.
- *Several Class Sessions of "Reinforcement" and "Extension" Work.*   Students spend several class sessions in reteaching and reinforcement, or enrichment and extension work, depending on whether their performance on the assessments has met the established standard. Successful completion of extension work to a high standard, or assisting classmates to achieve at the required level of performance (so that those students are now eligible for a B grade) makes a student eligible for a grade of A. The time spent on reinforcement offers students who need more time the opportunity to consolidate their understanding and bring their performance up to the required standard. It is not a punitive step. It acknowledges that students learn at different rates but that all students are capable of achieving the standard.
- *Extra Assistance Provided Through a System of Learning Support for Those Who Require It.*   If students have not yet achieved the required standard of performance even after the period of reinforcement and review, they are eligible to receive additional assistance through the school's system of learning support: before or after school, during study hall, and so on. When they have achieved the required level, their grade is changed from Incomplete to B.

In summary, the gold standard for grading recognizes only three grades: A, B, and Incomplete. A grade of B indicates that the student has achieved the required standard of performance on the learning outcomes. A grade of A indicates that the student has completed rigorous additional assignments that demonstrate learning at a higher level or that the student has provided essential assistance to a classmate who, as a result of that assistance, can now perform at the required standard and is eligible for a grade of B. Other students receive an Incomplete, which indicates that they have not yet achieved the standard but that they are eligible for a B as soon as they have done so.

This system of grading creates a partnership between the teacher and students; the standards are well known to the students in advance of any assessments, and the teacher's role is to serve as a coach to help all students reach those standards. It also places students in charge of their own learning, encouraging them to engage in self-assessment and monitoring and to seek additional assistance when they need it.

COMMENTARY ON THE INSTRUCTIONAL EXAMPLES

The instructional examples demonstrate how teachers can incorporate student learning in an approach to grading.

How Many Beans?

While circulating and watching students tackle the estimation problem, the teacher can monitor students' computational proficiency and development of reasoning skills in thinking through the different approaches to the problem. By circulating and talking with students as they work, the teacher can ascertain the extent to which they are able to apply their computation skills to the problem and engage in two- or three-step problem solving.

The teacher is also able to assess the extent to which every student is contributing to the group's solution; it is important that some students' shaky understanding not be permitted to be hidden in the energy of group work. Thus, conversations with individual students about their strategies are important in order to gauge each student's understanding and to provide on-the-spot teaching as needed.

It is, of course, the individual student responses to the unit test that provide the teacher with solid information on the students' understanding of the process and limitations of estimation. In assessing student responses, teachers would look for:

- Selection of an appropriate method to attack the problem—for example, using the concept of area to divide a photograph of a crowd into 1-inch squares.
- Development of a suitable strategy for applying the method—for example, describing a method that involves counting the number of people in one square and multiplying that number by the number of squares.
- An explanation of the limitations of the method—for example, that not all parts of the photograph are equally crowded, so that some squares have fewer people than others.

Since this is an elementary class, it is not important for teachers to award a grade for this unit of work. However, it is important that the teacher be able to determine whether each student understands the basic principles of the unit: the range of possible strategies, the limitations of estimation, and the application of computation skills in a two- or three-step problem.

Pre-Revolutionary America

Students participating in the U.S. history unit provide the teacher with multiple opportunities to assess their understanding and proficiency in the many instructional outcomes in the unit. In generating questions, selecting a question to investigate, and doing research to answer that question, students demonstrate their conceptual understanding and reasoning skills.

The group presentations offer the teacher evidence of the students' understanding of the facts of the pre–Revolutionary War period and of the relationships among the different groups involved in the struggle. Their questions about the presentations of their classmates also provide multiple indications of how well students have grasped some of the bigger issues involved in the decision to attend the second Constitutional Congress and to sign the Declaration of Independence.

The students' performance on the test and their independent essays about the findings of their investigation demonstrate their understanding of what they have learned, independently of the work of their classmates. These efforts must be evaluated by the teacher using the criteria and scoring guides he or she has created. Proficient performance on these measures, combined with the assessments obtained through informal means, results in a grade of B. Those students whose work is not yet up to the required standard have additional time, with both teacher and peer assistance, to reach the necessary standard; when they do so, they also receive a B. And those students who challenge themselves with an additional small project, or who serve as a tutor to a classmate who is still reaching proficiency, are eligible for a grade of A.

Part 4

NONCLASSROOM RESPONSIBILITIES

Chapter 12 Fulfilling Professional Responsibilities
Chapter 13 Moving Toward Leadership

Most of the essential work of teaching occurs in the classroom; indeed, the popular view of teaching as involving the interaction between teacher and students is accurate. Teachers cannot achieve good results with their students if they have not perfected the skill of designing engaging learning experiences for them, experiences that respect the backgrounds of their students and lead them to important learning.

But to think that work in the classroom with students constitutes the whole of teaching is naive; there is also much behind-the-scenes work with colleagues, in addition to communicating with families. Furthermore, as teachers become more experienced, they tend to branch out beyond the classroom and to assume leadership roles, both formal and informal.

Part 4 describes, first of all, the important responsibilities involved in participating in a professional community. These responsibilities are both wide-ranging and essential. In fact, when teachers' performance is found to be below the acceptable standard, frequently it is aspects of their performance outside the classroom that are deficient: They have been unresponsive to parents or uncooperative with colleagues. These matters have an important effect on a teacher's effectiveness, because relationships with the adults in an educational environment have an enormous impact on a teacher's overall proficiency.

In addition, there is much work in a school that must be done by teachers but that is beyond the responsibility of individual teachers working with their own students. Decisions must be made about the curriculum, about common assessments, and about policies affecting students (such as grading and attendance) that are implemented schoolwide. In addition, many teachers find that they can make a contribution in designing or coordinating a new program for students, such as a chess club or a tutoring service in the community. Furthermore, some teachers find that they can help their school by forging a partnership with a local business, community agency, or university. These relationships are important to the overall life of the school and enhance the opportunities for students. In order to create them, teachers must assume a leadership role with their colleagues.

Chapter 12

Fulfilling Professional Responsibilities

The heart of teaching is, of course, the interactive work with students in the classroom. Noneducators, when they contemplate a teachers' work, think immediately and rightly of a teacher presenting information, explaining a concept, or leading a class discussion. A teacher who cannot engage students in important learning cannot be considered skilled.

But the interactive work is not all of teaching; indeed, there is much behind-the-scenes work as well. Some of this is planning, which has been addressed in Part 2, "Using What We Know to Promote Learning," in which the processes of getting to know one's students, determining worthwhile learning outcomes and assessments, and designing learning activities are described.

But planning does not constitute all of a teacher's nonclassroom responsibilities. These also entail professional work in the school and beyond: working with colleagues, communicating with parents, and engaging in serious and ongoing professional learning. These aspects of teaching are described in this chapter.

PARTICIPATING IN A PROFESSIONAL COMMUNITY

Schools are organizations that consist of committed professionals working both individually and collectively to do important and difficult work. Both aspects of this work are important: Educators have an individual responsibility to continue to improve their instructional skills, but they also must join with their colleagues to maximize the effectiveness of the school as a whole.

Individual Professional Learning

Teaching is extraordinarily complex work about which no educator ever stops learning. Ongoing study is therefore part of the professional obligation of every teacher. Every year brings us new approaches and variations on old approaches; they all deserve careful consideration and, if warranted, inclusion in one's repertoire. And although the fundamental principles of learning don't change (students construct their understanding from their own actions and their reflections on those actions), thoughtful teachers are always inventing new ways to help students achieve understanding. Thus, reading professional literature, attending courses and workshops, and trying new approaches in one's own classroom are essential components of a committed teacher's professional life.

Ongoing teacher learning includes, naturally, enhancing one's skill in instruction and in engaging students in important learning. In addition, however, many teachers find that they must continue learning about their subjects themselves. For example, the fields of biology and chemistry have undergone profound transformation in the past few decades, and additions are constantly made to children's literature. Just keeping up can present a formidable challenge for many teachers.

Furthermore, the field of electronic technology continues to expand. Although early computer applications are now implemented so widely that they may be considered as basic as using a pencil, others are created every day. Without constant vigilance, it's easy for teachers to find themselves left behind not only their colleagues, but even (and perhaps especially) their students. Of course, careful judgment is needed; a new technology that offers new "bells and whistles" might not be suitable for our purposes. But we can't determine whether a particular application is appropriate if we don't understand it. Hence, continuing technology updates are an important component of every teacher's ongoing program of professional development.

Collective Professional Learning

Every teacher has a professional obligation to continue learning. Although the learning is, of necessity, individual, the setting may be collective. That is, teachers may enroll in a weekend course or read professional journals; these efforts are important and are made individually. Most teachers find, however, that the professional learning they embark on with their colleagues is even more rewarding than that undertaken on their own.

Collective approaches to professional learning take many forms, from joint planning to study groups to a more formal version of lesson study. It is well known that schools include many experts: teachers who understand their subjects deeply, those who have a solid working knowledge of different instructional approaches, and those who succeed in enlisting students in taking on difficult learning. If teachers are treated as, and consider themselves to be, independent contractors in their work, then their expertise remains private and they are never able to take advantage of the expertise of their colleagues.

Teachers need one another's skills, experience, and insights as they go about the essential work of improving their practice. Furthermore, sharing expertise is not simply a matter of an experienced teacher passing along his or her "tricks of the trade" to a less experienced colleague (although that may be part of the process). More fundamentally, collective professional development involves teachers working together to solve their individual and shared problems and challenges. "How should I introduce this unit on the French Revolution?" "What approach would help students understand the concept of a prime number?" "How can I help students see the freedom that Jim represents for Huck Finn?" These are questions that stimulate discussion and sharing of practice: They don't have a single right answer, as many approaches are possible. Indeed, the questions themselves might be subject to challenge, such as "What makes you think that Jim *does* represent freedom for Huck?"

The professional conversations that follow such queries are rich, inviting teachers to share their own students' work and their students' experiences in learning difficult content. From these conversations emerges a shared and deep understanding of learning and teaching, resulting in enhanced intellectual capital of the school as a whole. The insights obtained are not the consequence of a "master" teacher guiding others; rather, they are the result of joint sharing and problem solving. Of course, there is a role for expertise; otherwise, such meetings become exercises in the "blind leading the blind." But the expertise may come from any source; although teachers with many years' experience have much to draw on, a less experienced teacher may also have important insights. And anyone on the faculty can bring a professional article to the table for conversation, inviting colleagues to explore how its insights might contribute to teachers' practice.

Contributing to the School

Most teachers, whether they actively choose it or not, find themselves involved in responsibilities that extend beyond their own classrooms. Committees need members from across the school or district, and many teachers feel an obligation to their students to sponsor a club or activity or to organize, for example, a toy drive for a local charity. Indeed, in many schools, such activities are expected of all teachers.

When they are new to teaching, most teachers find their hands full with their own classroom responsibilities. They have lessons to prepare (and then revise), student work to examine, and projects to organize. Classrooms are complex places, and keeping things moving forward is a large responsibility. Most teachers new to the profession don't have much time or energy left over for larger school or district projects.

However, as they gain experience, most teachers find that they are able to make a contribution to the larger effort. They decide that the school's policies on, for example, grading or homework are important to them in their own teaching and for the culture of the school, and they get involved in an effort to revise them. Alternatively, they recognize that the curriculum or the assessments they use are critical to their own effectiveness, and they devote time and energy to improving them. Every school requires the active professional engagement of teachers; those who can devote time and energy to shared projects make a significant contribution to the overall effort.

COMMUNICATING WITH PARENTS AND GUARDIANS

Parents care deeply about the progress of their children in school, and teachers must keep them informed. This communication spans many different aspects of the instructional program and makes a material contribution to the learning of individual students. The issue of culture is an essential subtext of all such communications. Particularly when teachers come from a different cultural or linguistic group than their students, attention to how information is received and understood is critical. Although some parents may appear very shy or reticent, they are simply demonstrating respect for what they regard as the natural authority of the school and the teacher. Alternatively, some parents may discourage their children (particularly their daughters) from challenging what they read in a textbook or something a teacher has said. Such reticence must be respected for what it is, a reflection of a deeply held cultural norm of deference.

Some parents remember their own negative experiences in school and avoid the school altogether. They may operate on the theory that the less contact they have the better, and they may therefore be reluctant to attend events at the school or even to come to parent-teacher conferences. In these situations, teachers must make a deliberate effort to reach out, to show reluctant parents that they are welcome, that their children are valued members of the class, and so on.

There are several related, though distinct, aspects of a teacher's responsibilities in communicating with families; these are described below.

Information About the Instructional Program

It's important for families to understand the basic shape of the instructional program. Most parents don't care to know the details of, for example, the third-grade curriculum, but they appreciate being informed of the major thrust of the year's work in reading or science. Thus, a summary of the topics to be studied during the year or, at the secondary level, a course syllabus is a welcome document for parents, either distributed in hard copy or posted on a Web site.

Most schools have procedures for communicating formally with parents about the instructional program, such as a "back-to-school night" at the beginning of the school year. Parents typically spend a little time with each of their children's teachers to receive an overview of the teacher's intentions for the year, to be informed of the teacher's approach to grading, and so on. Such events also provide an opportunity for parents to share information about their children that would not warrant a full conference.

Some teachers (particularly at the elementary level) produce a weekly newsletter describing events in the classroom, visitors who have been there, and activities that could be done at home. Students themselves can contribute to these efforts, thus playing an important role both in keeping their families up-to-date and in developing pride in their classroom.

Another technique used by many teachers is to send portfolios of work home with students, with instructions for them on how to review their contents with their parents. When they hear their children describe their work with pride and see the complexity of what they are doing, parents gain an increased appreciation of the program. A variation on this approach is the student-led conference, a meeting in the school at which students describe to their parents what they have been learning and show them the contents of their portfolio. As a result of these conferences, parents come to understand the program far better than they could simply from a brief paragraph in a curriculum document.

Information About Student Progress

Parents care deeply about the progress their children are making in school. They recognize that education represents their children's best opportunity for a secure and rewarding future, and they want them to be able to make the most of it. Fortunately, every school has well-established procedures for communicating this information to parents.

However, many parents may need to have the information interpreted. What does a grade of B actually mean? (Or S or NI?) Many parents may also wonder whether the grades given by a teacher are absolute or relative to each child's level. How does language acquisition fit into the issue of grading? If a student has been struggling to learn, modest progress might represent an enormous gain, but that same progress might be below expectations for another student who is further along in his or her learning. Alternatively, if a student is making steady progress in mathematics while simultaneously learning English, that might represent a significant increase in learning, whereas that same amount of progress in another student, whose native language is English, would be less remarkable.

Parents also care about other aspects of their children's performance. Are they making a good effort in school or do they tend to ignore the teacher's assignments? Do they demonstrate pride in their work? Do they cooperate with their classmates? These are aspects of a child's learning that rarely find formal expression in a school's grading system, yet they are issues about which parents understandably care deeply. They recognize that such characteristics and dispositions can influence their children's success in life even more than some of their academic achievements.

The traditional method used by many schools to keep parents abreast of their children's progress, in addition to report cards, is parent-teacher conferences. These are almost universal in elementary schools but less widespread at the secondary level. Typically, students are dismissed early on one or two days, and parents come to the school at a time appointed for a conference with their child's teacher(s). These sessions are usually brief— 20–30 minutes each—but they may be used to review important aspects of children's progress in school.

Some parents find it difficult to attend meetings at school, particularly if they are scheduled during the workday. For this reason, many schools arrange for at least some parent-teacher conferences to be held in the evening. And although this practice is important, it may not be enough for some parents, who have younger children at home to care for. Therefore, many schools offer child care at school during parent-teacher conferences so that parents can be assured that their younger children are safe while they are meeting with their older children's teachers.

Communication about students' progress is most successful when it is two-way. When a child demonstrates a new skill or understanding at home, such as reading a book before bed, it is helpful for parents to send word of this development to the child's teacher. Similarly, when parents observe their child struggling to understand a homework assignment, the teacher should hear about it; only through clear communication and a high level of trust between the school and the home can such information be shared.

Engagement of Families in the Instructional Program

It is sometimes possible for parents to take an active role in their children's education. Such engagement not only helps students make progress in their learning, it also contributes to the relationship between the school and the home. Parents become more informed about the school's program, and with familiarity comes understanding and appreciation.

Teachers use many different approaches to engage families. Some teachers suggest books to be read at bedtime or even lend them to families from the class or school library. Other teachers suggest learning tasks (such as setting the table or sorting laundry) that can be done at home in the course of normal household routines or games for road trips. Such suggestions can enrich the interaction between children and their parents; most parents are quite willing to accept them when they recognize their value. Alternatively, teachers of older students might ask them to interview a relative to gain insight into a historical period or the experiences of recent immigrants.

FULFILLING PROFESSIONAL OBLIGATIONS

Every school makes demands of its teachers, including when they are expected to arrive at school in the morning, when grade reports are due, the schedule of faculty and team meetings, and the like. Some of these are spelled out in negotiated agreements; others are simply a matter of the school's culture.

Professional norms are important in the life of a school; they clarify what is expected of teachers, eliminating ambiguity. But just as important, they clarify what teachers expect of one another so that teachers know when their colleagues are not fulfilling their obligations. Such norms set the tone for a school and for teachers' interactions with one another.

Ethics plays an important role in teachers' professional obligations. Educators must display honesty and integrity; others must be able to trust them to work in the best interests of students and the school as a whole, without consideration for their own convenience. Ethical educators maintain the confidentiality of students and colleagues, enabling others to trust them in their interactions.

Professional teachers are keenly aware of the interests of their students, particularly those who traditionally have been underserved by the school. They work as advocates for students, locating resources when needed in the school or in the larger community. They are alert to signs of physical abuse, and of drug or alcohol dependency, and are aware of how to handle situations with delicacy.

Professional teachers are fully engaged in the life of the school and can be trusted to adhere to high ethical standards in their interactions with students, parents, and colleagues.

They base their decisions and recommendations for action on the best interests of the community at large and on the needs of students, never on self-serving considerations. And if other teachers grumble about a school regulation, they either use their powers of persuasion to convince them of the need for the regulation or they work to change it. But part of being a professional is not to work in an underhanded or suspicious manner.

Professional teachers, in other words, are *professional;* they adhere to high professional and ethical standards. An important consequence of this stance is that when such a teacher makes a recommendation, colleagues can trust that the recommendation is considered and ethical and not undermined by self-serving considerations.

Summary

Teaching involves much work that is done behind the scenes, unobserved by students and parents. It involves a great deal of planning, locating of resources, and collaboration with colleagues on problems of practice. It is precisely the nonclassroom part of teaching that ensures its professional status; teachers are not merely following a script or a recipe. They are the experts regarding their own students and the subjects they teach. They make hundreds of decisions each day to enhance their practice for the benefit of their students. These decisions, and the knowledge on which they are based, constitute the heart of professionalism.

Chapter 13

Moving Toward Leadership

Engaging students in important learning, and honing the skills necessary to do so, represents a career-long endeavor. Committed teachers never finish their professional education; they continue learning throughout their lives. Indeed, teaching well is so complex that conscientious teachers find that they can devote professional energy throughout their careers to improving their techniques, working with colleagues, and achieving better results.

However, although learning to teach well can consume an entire career, some teachers, once they have become truly proficient, are eager to extend their influence beyond their classroom walls; they strive to exert a greater impact on the profession than they can achieve by practicing in a single classroom. These teachers are inclined to move into leadership roles, either formally or informally.

ADMINISTRATIVE LEADERSHIP

The traditional method by which teachers move up the ladder of professional responsibility is to become an administrator. Indeed, the term *educational leader* connotes for most people an administrator, either at a school or in a district office. The work of administrators is critical to the mission of schools.

Administrators are the ones who set the tone, establishing and maintaining the school's culture. They ensure that all members of the school community—students, teachers, non-instructional staff, formal and informal teacher leaders—are focused on the essential purpose of the school: to ensure high-level learning on the part of every student. They also provide essential administrative support for the important professional work of the school: seeing to the master schedule, arranging for teachers to have time for collegial work, and ensuring that the budget reflects the school's priorities. But unfortunately, in recent years the work of the site administrator has become almost impossible, with multiple and sometimes conflicting pressures exerted by a variety of sources.

Cultural Leadership

When educators contemplate a new initiative in their schools, especially when it is one they believe might be difficult to implement, the reason cited typically centers on the issue of culture and frequently on the matter of trust. When schools are run as top-down, authoritarian organizations in which teachers have little voice, the environment is not conducive to trying new approaches and taking risks. Such a "play-it-safe" culture does not lend itself to important professional work.

Furthermore, the work of teaching is highly complex, and traditionally some students, particularly minorities and children of poverty, have been poorly served by schools. To end the acceptance of inadequate performance by some students requires an environment of high expectations for teachers as well as students. Although teacher leaders play an essential role, the tone of this environment must be established and maintained by administrative leaders.

Administrators are the instructional leaders of their schools; they must have sufficient expertise to fully appreciate the challenges their teachers face and to guide the instructional program. However, they cannot be experts in every aspect of teaching, particularly in disciplines or at grade levels with which they have no personal experience. They must understand the big ideas and be capable of helping teachers address the issues that inevitably arise.

But they also must respect, and find ways of enabling, teachers who may be the true experts in their fields.

Practical Leadership

Schools are complex organizations, and leading them requires great skill in coordinating multiple events, different perspectives, and diverse priorities. Site administrators must see to it that the master schedule is prepared, which involves coordinating the work of many different teachers' workloads and preferences. In addition, the budget must be developed and monitored to reflect the priorities of the school, and its management must be transparent. Schools are part of a larger district with its own demands and priorities; managing a school within the context of a district requires skills of communication and negotiation to ensure that one's own school receives its share of resources and that educators from across the district can work together when that is advantageous.

In addition, the principal is the official voice of the school and must represent the school to parents, the business community, and the public in general. If there is a new initiative to be explained to parents or a partnership with a local business or community organization to be arranged, it is the principal who must do it. Teachers can play an important, even a critical, role, but the site administrator must be involved to provide the official sanction for the initiative.

Unfortunately, the role of school principal has become virtually impossible for a single individual to perform well. Increased accountability for results (usually as measured by state-mandated assessments) has put enormous pressure on principals to achieve short-term improvements in test scores. The increased diversity of the student body has, in many schools, intensified this challenge. Although most educators gladly accept the responsibility for improved results in student learning, they also experience enormous pressure when obliged to restrict their instruction to those subjects that are tested on state assessments; much valuable content is lost. In such an environment, and as the "point person" for accountability requirements from both state and federal government, many principals simply don't have the time or energy to help their faculties engage in sustained school improvement efforts.

TEACHER LEADERSHIP

Educators have long recognized the need to spread the leadership load among many individuals in the school. Administrators simply cannot perform all the leadership functions that a school requires, nor are they in the best position to do so. The challenging professional work of joint planning, lesson study, and collaborative review of student work is best done by teachers working together.

What Is Teacher Leadership?

Teacher leadership refers to the fact that certain teachers, sometimes on their own initiative and sometimes within a more formal structure, decide that they want to extend their influence beyond the students with whom they work every day. Their vision extends beyond their own classroom and perhaps beyond even their own instructional team or department.

They recognize the school for the complex system it is and see that students' experience in school is a function of more than their interaction with individual teachers; it is influenced by the *systems* in place in the school. This awareness can lead to professional restlessness, which then becomes what some teachers have described as a leadership "itch": the desire to reach out beyond their own classrooms.

In many settings, the only way for teachers to extend their influence is to become an administrator. But many teachers recognize that this is not the right avenue for them; they see themselves as *teachers,* and they know that the job of administrator entails work that does not particularly interest them. In fact, some teachers make the change to administration, only to return to teaching because they find that it suits them better. However, they still have the urge to exert a wider influence in their schools and on the profession. The concept of teacher reflects this desire to have a broader impact on the lives of the students in their schools.

Why Teacher Leadership?

Why do some teachers emerge as leaders and others do not? And what is the value of leadership to the schools of which they are a part? There are a number of contributing factors.

- *Teaching Is a "Flat" Profession.*   Teaching is one of the few professions in which the responsibilities of the 20-year veteran are essentially the same as those of the novice. In most other professions, as one gains experience, one has the opportunity to exercise greater responsibility and assume bigger challenges. This is not true of teaching, and it accounts for some of the itch that experienced teachers report. If unsatisfied, this urge for greater responsibility can lead to premature cynicism when teachers conclude that things will never change.
- *Teacher Tenure in Schools Is Longer Than That of Administrators.*   In many settings, administrators remain in their positions for only 3–4 years. There are exceptions, of course, but in general, teachers remain in their schools for longer periods. They hold the institutional memory; they are the custodians of the institutional culture. This suggests that if a school district is trying to make significant improvements in its schools, cultivating and encouraging teacher leaders may be a wise investment. They are in a position to take the long view, that is, to initiate long-range projects.
- *The Impossible Principalship.*   The literature on the principalship is vast; its very scope suggests the multiple demands of the position. As noted above, principals are expected to be competent managers (maintaining the physical plant and submitting budgets on time), visionary leaders (instilling a sense of purpose in their staff), instructional leaders (able to coach teachers in the nuances of classroom practice), and responsive to multiple stakeholders (parents, staff, the central office, and the larger community). It is virtually impossible for a single individual to possess all the necessary skills for such a complex role. Furthermore, the principal has become the point person for accountability requirements imposed by states and the federal government. Because they are under so much pressure from such a wide range of sources, many administrators simply cannot devote the time or energy required for continuing school improvement.
- *Limitations on Principal Expertise.*   Because of the enormous scope of the position of site administrator, the skills needed for instructional leadership are complex;

most principals, like all educators, have their areas of expertise. If a principal is a former math teacher, she may know a lot about instructional practices in mathematics but not in world languages. Similarly, a former second-grade teacher may be highly skilled in literacy development but less so in teaching science. This is not an indictment; it is simply a statement of reality. It's impossible for administrators to be expert in everything. But sustained school improvement entails implementing research-based practices. Many teacher leaders are more familiar with these practices in their field than their administrators can be.

The implications of these factors are profound; findings suggest that in order for student achievement to improve significantly, the responsibility can't rest on site administrators alone. Teachers must play a significant role in enhancing the profession. School improvement is not something *done to* teachers; it is something teachers *do.* This can happen in both formal and informal ways.

Types of Teacher Leadership

There are two fundamental types of teacher leaders: formal and informal. They are considerably different from one another in all ways, including how they are identified, what they do, and their position in the authority hierarchy of the school.

FORMAL TEACHER LEADERSHIP

Formal teacher leaders are those who are selected to play formal roles in the school, whether it is department chair, team leader, master teacher, or instructional coach. These individuals typically apply for their positions and are chosen through a selection process. Ideally, they also receive training for their new responsibilities. Generally speaking, the formal leadership roles performed by teachers constitute the important professional dialogue of the school. These roles are established; teachers typically apply for them (although they could rotate), and they frequently entail a reduced teaching load.

Department Chair

In many secondary schools, a member (typically the most senior member) of a department is designated as department chair, and these individuals, together with the principal, constitute the school's *leadership team.* In most schools, department chairs teach classes, although usually with a reduced class load. They may, for example, teach four classes each day rather than five. With the extra time at their disposal, department chairs are expected to ensure that the teachers in their departments have the equipment and supplies they need; that the teachers engage, where appropriate, in joint course, unit, and lesson planning; and that they create viable common assessments. This is important professional work, and it involves teachers working intensely with one another under the guidance of a colleague who is steeped in their discipline.

In some schools, department chairs are also asked to be involved in teacher evaluation. This ensures that content expertise is incorporated into that process. Many secondary teachers find that their practice is being evaluated by an administrator whose own content expertise may be in a different field, thus compromising the value of the evaluation process. However, when department chairs serve as evaluators, the relationship between them and the other teachers in the department changes dramatically. The department chair is no longer simply a colleague; he or she is also a judge.

Thus, a principal must decide how to deploy the skills of department chairs. Their content expertise is invaluable, of course; knowing a lot about a discipline and how to teach it is the way department chairs contribute to the collective understanding of a high school department. In an informal way, by visiting classrooms and meeting with teachers, department chairs can influence how a discipline is taught. But if they are also asked to evaluate their colleagues, the relationship between them changes; some teachers, feeling insecure in their work, tense up when the department chair enters their classroom. Thus, the department chair is unable to be the instructional resource intended by the school's administrator; on the other hand, site administrators also don't receive assistance in the supervisory work that they might have wanted. These are important trade-offs; each school must determine for itself the best way forward.

Team Leader

At the elementary and middle school levels, formal teacher leaders frequently serve as team leaders of, for example, the third-grade teachers. Because of the realities of scheduling, it is rare for team leaders to have a reduced teaching load. Furthermore, their roles rarely include supervisory responsibilities. Typically, an elementary or middle school team leader sits on the school's leadership team, serving as a communication conduit for issues with school-wide implications. Team leaders also coordinate team logistical matters, from coordinating field trips to ordering supplies and organizing joint team efforts such as parent presentations. Ideally, team leaders also play an instructional leadership role, coordinating the team's joint curriculum and lesson planning, lesson study, and analysis of student work.

Because of the rich possibilities for a leadership role of team leaders, it's important for them to receive training for their positions. This training can help them understand how to facilitate team meetings, plan joint lessons, and coordinate their common assessments. Without training for their role, many team meetings at the elementary and middle school levels revert to discussions of immediate concern, such as determining the route for the Halloween parade, rather than discussion on instructional matters.

Instructional Coach and/or Mentor

Many schools are able to invest in the roles of instructional coach and/or mentor. Mentors typically work with teachers new to the profession. Instructional coaches, on the other hand, usually have a particular area of expertise, such as literacy or mathematics, and are available as resources for the entire faculty of a school.

Coaches and mentors play a very important role in the professional life of a school. Especially when they receive some training for their work, these educators support their colleagues in the complex work of teaching, spending time in classrooms offering feedback, and engaging in joint planning and analysis of student work. This is important work, and it includes activities that site administrators have neither the time nor the expertise nor, in some cases, the inclination to undertake. Yet, engaging with colleagues in the basic details of classroom practice is the heart of job-embedded professional development; teachers work together to solve the difficult issues of practice that can yield only to sustained, thoughtful attention.

INFORMAL TEACHER LEADERSHIP

Teacher leadership in schools consists not only of formal teacher leaders, but of informal ones as well. Informal teacher leaders, in contrast to their formal leader peers, emerge spontaneously from the teacher ranks. They are not selected; instead, they take the initiative to address a problem or institute a new program. They have no formal position and therefore no positional authority; their influence stems entirely from the respect they command from their colleagues through their expertise and practice.

Informal teacher leadership has been fully described in *Teacher Leadership That Strengthens the Profession* by Charlotte Danielson (2006).

What Do Teacher Leaders Do?

In emerging spontaneously, informal teacher leaders exhibit some important skills, values, and dispositions. Teacher leadership in a school setting entails mobilizing and energizing others with the aim of improving a school's teaching and learning. A hallmark of leadership, therefore, is that it entails taking initiative in collaboration with others. This has been well described by Michael Fullan (2001):

> The litmus test of all leadership is whether it mobilises people's commitment to putting their energy into actions designed to improve things. It is individual commitment, but above all it is collective mobilisation. (p. 9)

In addition, informal teacher leaders must gain the commitment of colleagues to their vision; they must convince others of the importance of what they are proposing and their general plan for addressing it. They are attentive to data and evidence of student learning; they focus on those aspects of the school's program that will yield important gains in student learning. They are respected for their own instructional skill and can build a consensus among even a diverse group of educators. In other words, informal teacher leaders see their role as extending beyond the walls of their own classrooms; they look around them and notice that some aspect of the school's program could be improved. They then set out to implement that improvement.

In order to accomplish their work, informal teacher leaders exhibit certain essential values and dispositions in their interactions with others. They are open-minded and respectful of the views of others. They display optimism and enthusiasm, confidence and decisiveness. They persevere, not permitting a setback to derail an important initiative they are pursuing. On the other hand, they are flexible and are willing to attempt a different approach when the first effort fails.

It should be noted that the skills of informal teacher leadership are not fundamentally different from those of teaching; teachers also must be experts in their fields, as well as persuasive, open-minded, flexible, and confident. But teacher leaders display these traits with their colleagues as well as their students, and they regard the entire school, not only their own class, as the proper setting for their work.

Areas of School Life in Which Leadership Is Exercised

Teachers, even highly accomplished teachers, exercise their skill within their classrooms. They work to improve the level of student engagement, the quality of student work, and the extent of student learning. Although they may collaborate with colleagues, they are working on behalf of their own students.

Informal teacher leaders, on the other hand, in addition to continually seeking to be more effective in the classroom, extend their reach beyond the classroom to the school and beyond the school to the district, the state, or the nation. They become involved in schoolwide efforts to improve opportunities for students, to strengthen practice, and to initiate new programs. Their extended reach encompasses several areas of school life, which are described below.

Schoolwide Policies and Programs

Schoolwide policies and programs include such things as student policies, for example, attendance, grading, and discipline. In influencing these policies, teacher leaders work to ensure that they reflect the school's mission and that they embody respectful interactions between students and staff and among students. Another category of schoolwide policies and programs consists of student programs, such as student tutoring, drug-free schools, or student leadership programs. Such student programs contribute materially to students' experience of school, enriching it far beyond the academic program alone. In fact, for many students, such programs are the most memorable part of school life. Teacher leaders play an active role in such programs, ensuring broad access to them.

Teacher leaders also contribute to school organization and structures, for example scheduling, budgeting, and decision-making processes. These systems form the skeleton of the school's operation, defining how the other parts interact. Teacher leaders take an active role in the school's governance, contributing to decisions regarding, for instance, the master schedule or policies on student enrollment in advanced courses. Moreover, they ensure that these decisions are made in a manner that reflects and contributes to the school's vision for learning and the student culture of hard work and success.

Lastly, teacher leaders play a pivotal role in organizing professional development offerings in the school. They work to ensure that these reflect principles of effective practice, such as being job embedded, and focus on identified needs. In addition, they cultivate, through these professional development programs, the school culture of professional inquiry.

Teaching and Learning

Informal teacher leaders help their colleagues focus on evidence of student learning and how it can be improved. That means that they have a keen eye for data of all types and what they reveal about both the quality of student learning, and the equity of access to high-level learning. They help others analyze student work and examine statistics in search of patterns indicating over- or underrepresentation of certain groups of students in various classes.

Teachers are, in many cases, the true experts regarding the subjects they teach and the most effective ways to teach them. And although the content standards for students may have been developed at the state or district level, decisions regarding the application of those standards to specific situations, with specific groups of students, are made at the school and classroom levels. Teacher leaders work with their colleagues to ensure that the resulting curriculum is rich and has been prepared with maximum coordination and integration across disciplines.

Student assessment is another area in which teacher leaders exert influence in the school, improving both formative and summative assessment to enhance learning opportunities for students. They ensure that school-based assessments are aligned with curriculum goals, that students have multiple ways in which to demonstrate their learning, and that teachers have the skill to use ongoing assessment in their classrooms.

Finally, teacher leaders promote excellent teaching in their schools. They recognize that teaching is both complex and important, and they seek ways to initiate new or coordinated approaches. This can entail many activities, from organizing a study group to explore a new approach to establishing a system for teachers to observe one another.

Communication and Community Relations

The last area of school life in which teacher leaders make a material contribution is that of communication and community relations. The first of these consists of family communication and involvement. Of course, all teachers communicate with the families of the students they teach. But in addition, there are schoolwide efforts (such as an information night regarding the new math program) that are best organized and presented by teachers to parents from across the school.

Schools also need systems for communicating with other educators so that the transition of students from one level of schooling to another is as smooth as possible. This sometimes takes the form of curriculum coordination or sharing of instructional approaches (for example, in the teaching of writing) or the development of efficient systems for sharing student portfolios.

In addition, many schools establish partnerships with public and private agencies, universities, and the business community to enrich the school's program for both students and teachers. Teacher leaders can play an active role in making these connections and linking resources with those who can use them.

SKILLS OF TEACHER LEADERSHIP

In their preparation programs, teachers learn the skills of teaching, engaging students in learning, managing the complex environment of classrooms, and communicating sensitively with the parents of their students. But the skills required for teacher leadership are fundamentally different, involving deep knowledge of the issues that might arise in work with colleagues: curriculum planning, assessment design, data analysis, and the like. Furthermore, the actual work of assuming leadership with colleagues—active listening, facilitating a meeting, keeping a group discussion on track, deciding on a course of action and monitoring progress—involves skills that are not typically taught in a program of teacher preparation. These skills go beyond a teacher's work in the classroom and, if a teacher leader is to be effective, must be developed.

Summary

For many teachers, the daily challenges of preparing for their students and engaging them in important learning produce a sufficient professional reward. But there are others, teachers who are interested in extending their influence beyond their own classrooms, who seek to play a leadership role in their schools. There are many options for these educators, from informal teacher leadership activities to more formal teacher leadership roles to administrative positions.

INSTRUCTIONAL EXAMPLES

HOW MANY BEANS? (INTERMEDIATE MATHEMATICS)

This is a brief unit, lasting for 4–7 days (depending on the amount of time devoted to it each day), in which students explore estimating large numbers, in this case by estimating the number of beans in a jar. They learn that there are many different approaches to this problem and that some are more accurate than others. In pursuing this investigation, students apply their computational skills in a practical situation. Thus, the investigation may be considered an opportunity to engage students in mathematical applications to an intriguing problem.

Learning Outcomes

By the completion of this unit, students will:

- Understand several different approaches to estimating large numbers (conceptual understanding)
- Create a logical solution to a multistep problem (reasoning skills)
- Apply computation skills to a practical situation (procedural knowledge)
- Appreciate that there are limits to all methods of estimation (conceptual understanding)
- Apply the skills of collaboration (collaboration skills)
- Make a presentation to classmates summarizing their findings (communication skills)

Materials Needed

- For each table:

    a pint or quart jar filled with beans

- For the class:

    several pan balances
    a number of small containers, such as portion cups
    large pieces of newsprint
    yard or meter sticks
    markers

Assessment Methodologies

- ***Formative.*** The teacher will circulate while students are working to monitor the quality of their thinking and the methods they are using. This will enable the teacher to collect anecdotal information on the students' reasoning and computation skills.
- ***Summative.*** Students will take a test in which they apply what they have learned to a new problem, such as estimating the number of people at a demonstration from an aerial photograph. As part of the written test, students will explain, in their own words, why they have adopted a particular approach and the limits to that approach.

Background

This unit is a brief exploration of the methods for estimating large numbers. It invites students to investigate several different methods for estimating the number of beans in a jar, compare those estimates with the actual number, and determine the most accurate and efficient methods.

The methods available for students to use are:

- *Weight.* They weigh, on a balance, a small number of beans, for example 25. Then they weigh all the beans in the jar and calculate the number of beans in the jar.
- *Volume.* They count the number of beans in a small portion cup, determine how many times the cup can be filled using the beans in the jar, and calculate the total.
- *Area.* They make a grid on a piece of newsprint and count the number of beans that cover a section of the grid. Then, by determining the number of sections covered by all the beans in the jar, they calculate the total.
- *Layers.* They count the number of beans in a "layer" in the jar and count the number of layers; they then calculate the number of beans in the jar by multiplying the number of layers by the number of beans in each layer.

In completing the activities in the unit, students put their skills of calculation to work in a practical setting. They are also exposed to the concepts of estimation and measurement error. None of the estimation methods will yield a result as accurate as that of actual counting; however, for many purposes, an estimate is good enough, and it is completed much more quickly than counting. Indeed, in some circumstances, counting is not even possible. Of course, the exploration will identify some approaches as being superior to others. However, the comparison is among the *methods,* not among the *students.* This distinction is critical and reinforces the nature of scientific and mathematical inquiry.

Learning Experiences

Note: the number of days devoted to this investigation is a function of the amount of time each day devoted to it. If students have only 30 minutes per day, for example, more days will be needed than if they have 45 minutes per day.

Day 1
Setting the problem

- Students sit at tables in groups (either established by the teacher or by student friendship groups).
- Teacher distributes the jars filled with beans to each table.
- Teacher presents the problem: how many beans are in the jar? How could you find out without counting each one?
- Students, in their table groups, consider different approaches.
- One student from each group reports the group's thinking.

Day 2
Exploration of alternatives

- Building on the previous day's discussion, the teacher summarizes the different estimation methods available to the students: weight, area, volume, and layers.

- Each table group selects one method to use, estimating the number of beans in the jar by that method. If they finish their work before the end of the time available, they can try a different method.
- Teacher circulates while the students are working to offer assistance as needed and to monitor their understanding.
- Teacher emphasizes, as needed, that the purpose of the exploration is to determine which *methods,* not which *students,* arrive at the most accurate estimate.

Day 3
Continuation of calculations

- If more time is needed for the activities from Day 2, students continue their investigations to arrive at an estimate of the number of beans in the jar.

Day 4
Explanation of methods used

- Student groups prepare a written explanation on newsprint of how they calculated their answer.

Day 5
Comparison of methods used

- One member of each group makes a brief presentation to the class of the method used by the group to determine the number of beans in the jar.
- The teacher records the estimates on the board, emphasizing the methods, not the students involved, in each estimate.
- Teacher invites the students to form hypotheses regarding the similarities or differences in the different estimates.

Day 6
Counting of beans

- In their table groups, students count the actual number of beans in their jars; the results are compared.
- Teacher conducts a discussion on why some methods seem to produce more accurate estimates than others.

Day 7
Assessment

- Teacher provides each student with a copy of a large number of objects of which they are to estimate the number; they write an explanation of how they would approach the task. One possible approach is to duplicate a newspaper photograph of a demonstration and ask students to estimate (as the police department or the organizers of the demonstration would want to do) how many people participated in it. They should answer these questions:

   Approximately how many people are in the demonstration?
   How did you arrive at your answer?
   Are there other methods you could have used? Why or why not?

THE PRE–REVOLUTIONARY WAR PERIOD IN U.S. HISTORY (HIGH SCHOOL SOCIAL STUDIES)

This unit is organized as an independent investigation by students of questions of their own formulation (with assistance by the teacher) and analysis of information, culminating in group presentations and the consolidation of information regarding the period. The unit satisfies the state's content standards relating to history, political systems, data analysis, technology, and oral and written communication.

Learning Outcomes

By the completion of this unit, students will:

- Know the events of the pre–Revolutionary War period (factual knowledge)
- Understand the critical differences between a monarchy and a republic (conceptual understanding)
- Formulate questions to be investigated (reasoning skills)
- Determine the evidence needed to answer important questions and locate that evidence (reasoning skills)
- Demonstrate appropriate and imaginative use of electronic technology in conducting investigations and making a presentation (procedural knowledge, reasoning skills)
- Analyze data regarding the pre–Revolutionary War period (reasoning skills)
- Understand the perspectives of different groups involved in the effort to achieve independence (dispositions, point of view)
- Work cooperatively with others (collaboration skills)
- Illustrate results through visual representation (reasoning skills; communication skills)
- Make a presentation to classmates summarizing findings (communication skills)
- Write a well-organized essay on the findings (communication skills)

Assessment Methodologies

- ***Formative.***   The teacher will be engaged with students throughout the unit, monitoring their developing skill in formulating focused questions, identifying evidence, conducting an investigation, analyzing data, and working collaboratively. He or she will provide feedback to students on an ongoing basis.
- ***Summative.***   By the conclusion of the unit, students will:

  Complete a unit test requiring both short-answer and essay answers
  Present part of a group report, with an established rubric for evaluation
  Write a reflective essay on what they have learned about the pre–Revolutionary War period from their own research and from their classmates
  Demonstrate skills of working with others

Note: because many of the learning experiences of this unit engage students in collaborative work, the evaluation of collaboration skills will consist of informal records kept by the teacher during student work sessions.

Day 1
Introduction

- Activity: signers of the Declaration of Independence (see detailed directions on page 143).
- Students formulate questions.
- Teacher and students create a web illustrating the relationships among the different questions.

Homework: Students consider the activity and the class discussion and formulate a question that interests them for further investigation. Guidelines for the homework assignment: "Consider the questions you heard today. Identify a question that you believe is important and that you would like to explore more thoroughly. Why do you think it's important?" Limit: 200 words.

Day 2
Focus on questions and identifying evidence

- Students share the questions they generated for homework and divide into groups of three or four students who were attracted to similar questions.
- Students, in their groups, focus their questions.
- Students determine what evidence would answer their questions and where they think they could find that evidence. They identify possible evidence on Worksheet 2.
- Students make a plan describing which members of their group will seek each piece of evidence.
- Teacher circulates, probing student thinking, helping to shape the questions so that they are researchable; serves as a resource to students in identifying evidence.

Homework: Students begin collecting evidence to answer the question they have selected.

Days 3–6
Investigations

- Students report on any difficulties they encountered in their first investigative efforts for homework; teacher facilitates a discussion to help students improve their approaches.
- Students conduct research in the library, online, and so on.
- Students prepare group presentations on their findings, referring to the presentation rubric previously developed by the class.
- Teacher serves as a resource for students in their investigations.

Homework for Days 3–5: Students continue their investigations after school, either in the school or community library or at home.

Homework for Day 6: Students write a summary essay of their own and their group's findings, following guidelines provided by the teacher. These guidelines should, to the extent possible, be the result of a collaborative effort between the teacher and the students.

Days 7–8
Presentations

- Students, in their groups, describe their findings to the class.
- Other students pose questions for their classmates as appropriate.

- Other students comment on the quality of their classmates' presentations, referring to the presentation rubric.
- Teacher and students identify relationships among the perspectives offered in the different presentations.
- Teacher distributes a study guide for the period, identifying essential questions.

Homework: Students read the chapter in the textbook, relating it to what they have learned from their own and other groups' investigations and findings. They prepare responses to study questions provided by the teacher.

Day 9
Closure

- Teacher leads a discussion with the class, pulling together threads from the different presentations and prompting the students in relating their findings to the textbook account and the study questions.

Homework: Students prepare for the unit test, using their own notes and the study questions prepared by the teacher.

Day 10
Unit test: some multiple-choice/short answer; two brief essays.

Learning Experiences

Day 1: Introduction and Initial Formulation of Questions
Note: a critical contributor to the success of this unit is the initial activity, in which students examine a list of the signers of the Declaration of Independence (Worksheet 1) and formulate questions based on information provided.

Examples of questions students might pose:

- How were people selected to participate in the Second Continental Congress (the body that adopted the Declaration of Independence)? Why were there so many more representatives from some colonies than others?
- Did delegates have to be wealthy to participate? Were they paid a salary or did they have to work as a public service, with no compensation or expenses paid?
- Were there any delegates at the Congress who declined to sign the Declaration of Independence?
- It appears that some of the delegates were related to one another (for example, the Lees). Were they brothers or brothers-in-law? Were any other delegates related to one another even though they didn't have the same name?
- Did some delegates' signing of the Declaration of Independence alienate members of their own families? Were any of them criticized or ostracized for this action?
- What were these people risking in signing the Declaration? Were they wealthy people? Would they have lost their property or even their lives? Were they concerned about this?

Day 1: Directions for the "Signers" Activity

Topic	Student Material	Task	Grouping	Teacher Role	Comments
Introduction		T provides context; reminds students of information from previous units about the situation in the various colonies.	Large group		
Generating questions	Worksheet: 1: Signers of the Declaration of Independence	T asks students to examine the worksheet, make observations about what they see, and generate questions. Then they should share their questions with others at their table.	Individuals Small groups	Provides an example of an observation and a question (for example, it appears that there were many delegates from Pennsylvania; I wonder if that's because Pennsylvania had the largest population of any of the colonies?). Provides information as appropriate, such as: "Remember that the people who signed this document were taking a big risk; they could have been hanged for treason if the colonies had not been successful in the war."	
Collecting questions	Flip chart	A representative from each table reports one of the group's questions, with the teacher noting them on a flip chart. Cluster similar ones together. Go around the group until all the questions are exhausted.	Large group	As questions are posed, the teacher helps students see the connections among different questions and places them in a larger social and cultural context. Ensures that all important areas are included in the students' questions; if not, pose them and invite student responses.	The teacher knows what facts and concepts can emerge from this study and has the responsibility to ensure that the questions that will be explored will include all important aspects of the period.

(continued)

Day 1: Directions for the "Signers" Activity (*continued*)

Topic	Student Material	Task	Grouping	Teacher Role	Comments
Clustering questions		Students are invited to examine the questions that have been proposed and to determine how they are related to one another (which ones are situated within other questions, etc.).	Table groups	Circulates while students are working to advise them on how they are interpreting the different questions.	
		Spokesperson from each table group gives a brief report on the group's work, and on how they interpreted the questions and their relationships to one another.	Large group	As appropriate, points out the similarities and differences among the different table groups' findings.	
Homework	Worksheet: An Interesting Question	Students reflect on the questions that have been generated during the class and determine one they would like to investigate, either on their own or with classmates.	Individuals		

Worksheet 1: Signers of the Declaration of Independence

Delegate and Colony	Vocation	Birthplace	Birth Date	Death Date
Adams, John (MA)	Lawyer	Braintree (Quincy) MA	10/30/1735	07/04/1826
Adams, Samuel (MA)	Political Leader	Boston, MA	09/27/1722	10/02/1803
Bartlett, Josiah (NH)	Physician, Judge	Amesbury, MA	11/21/1729	05/19/1795
Braxton, Carter (VA)	Farmer	Newington Plantation, VA	09/10/1736	10/20/1797
Carroll, Charles (MD)	Lawyer	Annapolis, MD	09/19/1737	11/14/1832
Chase, Samuel (MD)	Judge	Princess Anne, MD	04/17/1741	06/19/1811
Clark, Abraham (NJ)	Surveyor	Roselle, NJ	02/15/1726	09/15/1794
Clymer, George (PA)	Merchant	Philadelphia, PA	03/16/1739	01/23/1813
Ellery, William (RI)	Lawyer	Newport, RI	12/22/1727	02/15/1820
Floyd, William (NY)	Soldier	Brookhaven, NY	12/17/1734	08/04/1821
Franklin, Benjamin (PA)	Printer, Publisher	Boston, MA	01/17/1706	04/17/1790
Gerry, Elbridge (MA)	Merchant	Marblehead, MA	07/17/1744	11/23/1814
Gwinnett, Button (GA)	Merchant	Down Hatherly, England	c. 1735	05/19/1777
Hall, Lyman (GA)	Physician	Wallingford, CT	04/12/1724	10/19/1790
Hancock, John (MA)	Merchant	Braintree (Quincy), MA	01/12/1737	10/08/1793
Harrison, Benjamin (VA)	Farmer	Berkeley, VA	04/05/1726	04/24/1791
Hart, John (NJ)	Farmer	Stonington, CT	c. 1711	05/11/1779
Hewes, Joseph (NC)	Merchant	Princeton, NJ	01/23/1730	11/10/1779
Heyward, Thomas, Jr. (SC)	Lawyer, Farmer	St. Luke's Parish, SC	07/28/1746	03/06/1809
Hooper, William (NC)	Lawyer	Boston, MA	06/28/1742	10/14/1790
Hopkins, Stephen (RI)	Judge, Educator	Providence, RI	03/07/1707	07/13/1785
Hopkinson, Francis (NJ)	Judge, Author	Philadelphia, PA	09/21/1737	05/09/1791
Huntington, Samuel (CT)	Judge	Windham County, CT	007/03/1731	01/05/1796
Jefferson, Thomas (VA)	Lawyer	Shadwell, VA	4/13/1743	07/04/1826
Lee, Francis Lightfoot (VA)	Farmer	Westmoreland County, VA	10/14/1734	01/11/1797
Lee, Richard Henry (VA)	Farmer	Westmoreland County, VA	01/20/1732	06/19/1794
Lewis, Francis (NY)	Merchant	Llandaff, Wales	03/01/1713	12/31/1802
Livingston, Phillip (NY)	Merchant	Albany, NY	01/15/1716	06/12/1778
Lynch, Thomas Jr. (SC)	Farmer	Winyah, SC	08/05/1749	At sea, 1779
McKean, Thomas (DE)	Lawyer	New London, PA	03/19/1734	06/24/1817
Middleton, Arthur (SC)	Farmer	Charleston, SC	06/26/1742	01/01/1787
Morris, Lewis (NY)	Farmer	Morrisania (Bronx Co), NY	04/08/1726	01/22/1798
Morris, Robert (PA)	Merchant	Liverpool, England	01/20/1734	05/09/1806
Morton, John (PA)	Judge	Ridley, PA	1724	April, 1777
Nelson, Thomas Jr. (VA)	Farmer	Yorktown, VA	12/26/1738	01/04/1789
Paca, William (MD)	Judge	Abingdon, MD	10/31/1740	10/23/1799
Paine, Robert Treat (MA)	Judge	Boston, MA	03/11/1731	05/12/1814
Penn, John (NC)	Lawyer	Near Port Royal, VA	05/17/1741	09/14/1788
Read, George (DE)	Judge	Near North East, MD	09/18/1733	09/21/1798
Rodney, Caesar (DE)	Judge	Dover, DE	10/07/1728	06/29/1784
Ross, George (PA)	Judge	New Castle, DE	05/10/1730	04/14/1779
Rush, Benjamin (PA)	Physician	Byberry (Philadelphia), PA	12/24/1745	04/19/1813
Rutledge, Edward (SC)	Lawyer	Charleston, SC	11/23/1749	01/23/1800
Sherman, Roger (CT)	Lawyer	Newton, MA	04/19/1721	07/23/1793
Smith, James (PA)	Lawyer	Dublin, Ireland	c. 1719	07/11/1806
Stockton, Richard (NJ)	Lawyer	Near Princeton, NJ	10/01/1730	02/28/1781

(continued)

Worksheet 1: Signers of the Declaration of Independence (*Continued*)

Delegate and Colony	Vocation	Birthplace	Birth Date	Death Date
Stone, Thomas (MD)	Lawyer	Charles County, MD	1743	10/05/1787
Taylor, George (PA)	Ironmaster	Ireland	1716	02/23/1781
Thornton, Matthew (NH)	Physician	Ireland	1714	06/24/1803
Walton, George (GA)	Judge	Prince Edward County, VA	1741	02/02/1804
Whipple, William (NH)	Merchant, Judge	Kittery, ME	01/14/1730	11/28/1785
Williams, William (CT)	Merchant	Lebanon, CT	04/23/1731	080/2/1811
Wilson, James (PA)	Judge	Carskerdo, Scotland	09/14/1742	08/28/1798
Witherspoon, John (NJ)	Clergyman, Educator	Gifford, Scotland	02/05/1723	11/15/1794
Wolcott, Oliver (CT)	Judge	Windsor, CT	12/01/1726	12/01/1797
Wythe, George (VA)	Lawyer	Elizabeth City, VA	1726	06/08/1806

Day 2: Focusing Questions and Identifying Evidence

Topic	Student Material	Task	Grouping	Teacher Role	Comments
Formation of work groups		Students report on the question they identified for homework as interesting to explore; they form work groups accordingly.	Table groups	Assist students in recognizing the connections among the different questions and steer students to work groups that will enable them to explore questions they find interesting.	The teacher role's and at this stage is critical in helping students find a congenial group but also in ensuring that the questions being explored will yield information important to student understanding of the pre–Revolutionary War period.

The teacher also has a responsibility to ensure that the emerging groups will have the appropriate mix of students. |
| Identifying needed data | Worksheet: 2: Necessary Data | At each table, students select several of the questions to determine the data they will need to collect to answer the questions. | Table groups | Circulate while groups are working to provide assistance. | This activity is designed to provide an introduction to the idea of data collection. The teacher's role is important in helping students narrow their questions to ones that they can answer and that will prove to be interesting. |

Worksheet 2: Necessary Data

Directions: Select several questions that have been produced in class. Determine what information you would need to answer the questions and where you might find that information.

Question	Information	Information Source

ADDITIONAL RESOURCES

Barrell, J. (1991). *Teaching for thoughtfulness.* White Plains, NY: Longman.

Barrell, J. (2003). *Developing more curious minds.* Alexandria, VA: Association for Supervision and Curriculum Development.

Black, P., Harrison, C., Lee, C., Marshall, B., & William, D. (2004). Working inside the black box: Assessment for learning in the classroom. *Phi Delta Kappan, 86*(1), 8–21.

Boyer, E. (1983). *High school: A report on secondary education in America.* New York: Harper & Row.

Deci, E. (1995). *Why we do what we do.* New York: G. P. Putnam Sons.

Fogarty, R. (Ed.). (1998). *Problem-based learning: A collection of articles.* Arlington Heights, IL: Skylight Training and Publishing.

Fosnot, C. T. (1989). *Enquiring teachers; enquiring learners/A constructivist approach to teaching.* New York: Teachers College Press.

Ginnott, H. G. (1969). *Between parent and teenager.* New York: Macmillan.

Glasser, W. (1986). *Control theory in the classroom.* New York: Harper & Row.

Glasser, W. (2001). *Every student can succeed.* Chatsworth, CA: William Glasser, Inc.

Greene, D., & Lepper, M. (1974). How to turn play into work. *Psychology Today, 8*(4), 49–52.

Hertzberg, F, Mausner, B, & Snyderman, B. (1993). *The motivation to work.* New Brunswick, NJ: Transaction.

Hiebert, J., Carpenter, T. P., Fennema, E., & and Fuson, K. C. (1997). *Making sense: Teaching and learning mathematics with understanding.* Portsmouth, NH: Heinemann.

Jackson, D. B. (2003, April.). Education reform as if student agency mattered: Academic microcultures and student identity. *Phi Delta Kappan, 84*(8), 579–591.

James, W. (1983). *Talks to teachers on psychology.* Cambridge, MA: Harvard University Press.

Johnson, S. M. (1990). *Teachers at work: Achieving success in our schools.* New York: Basic Books.

Kohn, A. (1993). *Punished by rewards.* Boston: Houghton Mifflin.

National Research Council. (1999). *How people learn.* Washington, DC: National Academy Press.

Perkins, D. (1992). *Smart schools: From training memories to educating minds.* New York: Free Press.

Peters, T., & Austin, N. (1985). *A passion for excellence: The leadership difference.* New York: Warner Books.

Resnick, L. B. (1980).The role of invention in the development of mathematical competence. In R. H. Kluwe & H. Spadea (Eds.), *Developmental models of thinking* (pp. 213–244). New York: Academic Press.

Resnick, L. B., and Klopfer, L. E. (Eds.). (1989). *Toward the thinking curriculum: Current cognitive research.* Alexandria, VA: Association for Supervision and Curriculum Development.

Stigler, J. W., & and Hiebert, J. (1999). *The teaching gap.* New York: Free Press.

Taba, H., & Elzey, F. (1964). Teaching strategies and thought processes. *Teachers College Record, 65,* 524–534.

Von Glasersfeld, E. (1989). Cognition, construction of knowledge, and teaching. *Synthese, 80,* 121–140.

REFERENCES

Binet, A.(1975). *Modern ideas about children* (S. Heisler, Trans.). Menlo Park, CA: Susan Heisler. (Original work published 1909)

Black, P., Harrison, C., Lee, C., Marshall, B., & Wiliam, D. (2003). *Assessment for learning.* Philadelphia: Open University Press.

Bloom, B. (1984). The search for methods of group instruction as effective as one-to-one tutoring. *Educational Leadership, 41*(8), 4–17.

Chappius, J. (1975). Helping students understand assessment. *Educational Leadership, 63*(3), 39–43.

Danielson, C. (2006). *Teacher leadership that strengthens the profession.* Alexandria, VA: Association for Supervision and Curriculum Development.

deGrasse, Justice Leland. (2001, January 11). Excerpts from judge's ruling on school financing. *New York Times.* Retrieved August 25, 2008, from http://query.nytimes.com/gst/fullpage.html?res= 9D03E4DD1E3AF932A25752C0A9679C8B63.

Dewey, J. (1915). *The school and society.* Chicago: University of Chicago Press.

Dweck, C. S. (2000). *Self-theories: Their role in motivation, personality, and development.* Philadelphia: Psychology Press.

Dweck, C. S. (2006). *Mindset: The new psychology of success.* New York: Random House.

Friedman, T. (2007, June 10). Israel discovers oil. *New York Times.* Retrieved August 25, 2008, from http://select.nytimes.com/2007/06/10/opinion/10friedman.html?scp=1&sq=Friedman,%20T.%20 (2007,%20June%2010).%20Israel%20discovers%20oil&st=cse

Fullan, M. (2001). *Leading in a culture of change.* New York: Jossey-Bass.

Goleman, D. (1995). *Emotional intelligence.* New York: Bantam Books.

Guskey, T. (2003). How classroom assessments improve learning. *Educational Leadership, 60*(5), 6–11.

Kounin, J. S. (1977). *Discipline and group management in classrooms.* Huntington, NY: R. E. Krieger.

Piaget, J., & Inhelder, B. (1973). *Memory and intelligence.* New York: Basic Books.

Sergiovanni, T. J. (1992). *Moral leadership.* San Francisco, Jossey-Bass.

Shulman, L. S. (2004). *The wisdom of practice: Essays on teaching, learning, and learning to teach.* San Francisco: Jossey-Bass.

INDEX